Dear Mama

To Lois Staats—
Thank you for
your interest.

Dear Mama

The Krajicek Boys' Letters
To Their Runaway Mother

David J. Krajicek

News Ink Books

News Ink Books

Copyright 2020 by David J. Krajicek

ISBN 978-0-9849036-0-3

Original Illustrations by Karen Gutliph Graves

Book Design by Terry Bradshaw

Connie and Eddie Krajicek, circa 1933

In Memory of Conrad J. and Edward L. Krajicek

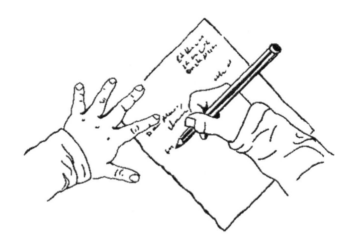

Mama, send me your picture if you can. That will be a birthday present from you to me. ~ Your loving son, Edward Krajicek

I sure wish that you would come home, mom. It would seem just grand to see you once again.—Love, Connie

Contents

Introduction

IN 1936, A NEBRASKA HOUSEWIFE named Hazel Chandler Krajicek walked out on her husband, Ed, and their two young sons, Eddie and Connie. She ran away to Michigan and never returned home. Her husband soon divorced her, and the boys saw their mother only occasionally for the rest of their lives.

Among the living, no one really knows the details of what prompted Hazel to leave her family. The principal parties to the tragedy — Ed, Hazel, and their sons — are all gone now. But among their survivors, the default explanation has always been Hazel's questionable morals and unquenchable thirst for alcohol.

When Hazel died in 1981, Eddie Krajicek traveled from Omaha to Gladwin, a north-central Michigan farm town, to attend her funeral. During that visit, one of Hazel's Michigan relatives handed him a small green suitcase. Inside he found a trove of nearly 75 letters that he and his younger brother had written to their mother. Hazel had begun saving the letters nearly five decades earlier. The oldest dated from 1937, months after she had abandoned her boys. Eddie and Connie wrote periodically throughout the 1930s and

'40s, as schoolboys growing into teenagers. Connie stopped writing after his 16th birthday. Eddie continued to correspond with his mother during his two-year stint in the Navy in 1946 and '47, just after World War II ended. His letters then paused for 30 years after he returned to Omaha from the service and got busy with a marriage that produced three children in its first four years. The collection concluded with a handful of notes that Eddie wrote to his mother in 1977, as her health was failing.

The letters were passed along to me, as my family's writer and historian. Edward Francis Krajicek was my grandfather, and Eddie (Edward Lee) was my father. That, of course, makes Hazel my grandmother, although I barely knew her. For nearly 20 years I have contemplated these letters, which offer valuable insight into my father's essential nature and his family's dynamics. I transcribed the letters long ago as part of my initial plan to share them with siblings and other relatives. I wrote a brief introduction designed to give a touch of context to the letters. That draft parroted my family's long-held position that Grandma Hazel was an irredeemable drunk and a wretch. That narrative made sense. After all, what sort of monstrous woman would flee her own flesh and blood, leaving her boys motherless at the ages of 9 and 7? She had clearly failed my father, grandfather, and uncle, so what does she deserve from me, as a representative of the family she abandoned?

* * *

I tried to convince myself that the letters should speak for themselves. I "finished" that original version of this project a decade ago but never shared it because I knew that my short-shrift treatment didn't do justice to these priceless letters, which open a window to my family's past. Over the years, I have now and then pulled a few of Connie and my dad's letters from the stack, organized by date, that I keep on a bookcase in my office. Nearly all of them are in their original envelopes, like fading time capsules. Most of the early letters are written in lead pencil, but the handwriting is perfectly legible. Both Krajicek boys wrote in neat Catholic school cursive, no doubt inspired by fully habited nuns weaponized with heavy wooden rulers.

The boys surely felt anger and resentment toward their mother, but they rarely expressed it in their letters. They often seemed more aloof than angry. Psychologists say that emotional distancing is common among children in such abruptly fractured homes — a defense mechanism to protect an already-broken heart, I suppose. But some letters do reveal the deep sadness and longing that Eddie and Connie felt — best expressed by the wrenching first letter in the collection, from July 1937, when Eddie writes that he wants no gift for his 10th birthday except a picture of his mother.

Hazel clearly felt a similar longing on some level. The letters suggest that she corresponded fairly frequently with the boys. (Unfortunately, if her letters were saved, they have been lost.) To his credit, their father made certain that Eddie and Connie corresponded with Hazel. Ed Krajicek believed that it was important for them to maintain a relationship with their mother, no matter what he thought of her. So he would sit his sons down at the dining room table until they had written a sufficient number of lines. At age 19, Eddie wrote to Hazel, *"Dad always did tell Connie and I to write you, but I guess we were too young to understand."*

Hazel tried to nourish a proxy connection from afar by encouraging her sons to visit her mother and sisters back home in South Omaha. The boys would report these visits to Hazel. As Connie wrote in one letter about Grace Chandler, his maternal grandmother, *"I've been going down to Granny's quite often lately. She looks fine and is in the best of health."*

Connie's early letters often featured comical but charming jockeying for Christmas or birthday presents. (Through their sons' postal diplomacy, Ed and Hazel occasionally shared the cost of Christmas or birthday gifts.) In 1938, at age 9, Connie sent Hazel this subtle gift idea: *"I have a friend named Henry Hartnett. He has a Streamline sled. He takes accordion lessons. I carry his accordion home for him and to school for him."* He had to wait two years, but Hazel sent Connie a red-and-black Artitone button accordion for Christmas in 1940. A few weeks later, Connie wrote in his typically unfiltered way, "I got the accordion all right but no book. Will you send me a book?" The letters make clear that Connie strived to keep up with an older brother that he idolized. He also gushed about various vague schemes with his pal "Sonny" Hartnett: *". . . we are going to buy some machinery and put it down his cellar and we can make lots of stuff."* Eddie was more reserved in his letters, but Connie's rawness brought out honesty. His anger and frustration showed, for example, when he quit his Catholic school's Safety Patrol because a nun sentenced him to write 2,000 "penances" for failing to wash his patrol belt. And in closing his accordion-seeking letter, he wrote this touching accidental ode: *"Love from Conrad to Mama. I love you. Be a good girl. Love me."*

At age 16, Connie began a letter by writing, *"Not hearing from you very often makes it very difficult for me to write."* But in the same note, he enthused, *"Oh! I forgot to tell you that I'm going steady with the most wonderful girl in the world."* That letter, sent three days after Christmas in 1945, was the last from Connie in Hazel's little green suitcase. This was his postscript, apparently the last words he wrote to her (or the last that she saved): *"P.S. I miss you mom."*

Eddie's letters sometimes displayed flashes of his brother's boyish enthusiasm. He raved about the sorts of little things that inspired him—a visit to a new public swimming pool, his successes in baseball, his favorite sport. Both boys often mentioned their Krajicek cousins, many of whom grew up within a few blocks of one another along 36th Street in South Omaha. *"Little Judy weighs ten and one-half pounds,*" Eddie wrote in 1938. "*She is two months old. She has black hair and dark eyes. We all love her very much.*" In the same letter, he revealed this big news to his mother: "*I joined Radio Orphan Annie's Secret Society Club. I have a secret club book and pin. I can read all the secret messages.*"

Sadly, these joyful moments were exceptions. My father often seemed to write out of a sense of duty. Since my very first reading of these letters, I have puzzled over his fidelity to Hazel. I understand why Connie cut himself loose from the tenuous maternal tether while still a teenager; I would have done the same thing. But some of us, like Connie, are reactive. My dad branched in a different direction. Perhaps due to childhood trauma, he grew into the sort of deeply disciplined person who strived to maintain control of his life and circumstances. And he did that, in part, by being more proactive than reactive. He was a planner. I sense that Eddie, deep in his soul, needed to keep up a relationship with Hazel, however strange it might have been, to bring a sense of order to his life. The letter-writing filled that need.

Eddie also functioned as his brother's keeper; he tried desperately to bring order and discipline to Connie's sometimes messy life, to limited effect. "*Mama, Connie is a bad boy,*" the 9-year-old Eddie wrote. "*He won't even go to Mass on Sunday.*" Ten years later while in the Navy, he wrote, "*Connie did not graduate from school so he is going to summer school. I guess he is kind of footloose yet. I'll get him on the ball though when I get home.*"

Eddie frequently tattled to his mother about Connie's behavior. I think it was a grieving boy's subtle attempt to press Hazel to mend their broken family: *See, mama, Connie needs you.* Yet Eddie never overtly made that plea. He obviously was confused about the situation as a young boy — anyone would be. But he made no demands of her. Instead, what I find again and again in the letters, from the first to the last, is kindness. He habitually apologized for writing infrequently, even during periods — early in his stretch in the Navy, for example — when he sent many letters.

"I'm sorry I didn't write sooner," he wrote in 1938. *"I suppose you don't think much of me because I haven't written to you for so long,"* he wrote in 1943. *"Well, I won't try to make up any excuses, but I'll promise to try real hard to write you regular."* He renewed his vow three years later: *"I feel very guilty when I think of how very seldom I write to you, but I promise I shall write more often in the future."* He also repeatedly promised to urge Connie to write to her — again, to limited effect.

Eddie was kind to Hazel in many ways, including several attempts to assuage her guilt. In 1946, he vowed to stand by his mother despite her paranoia about gossip in South Omaha. *"No one on Q Street or anywhere else could say anything that could make me stop loving you,"* he wrote.

* * *

Still looking for inspiration to refocus this project, in early 2020 I reread the dozen letters that my father sent Hazel during his two years of military service. These are the longest and most detailed letters from Hazel's little suitcase — probably because Eddie had more time than he knew what to do with. For much of his final year in the Navy, he was stationed at a military hospital in Pearl Harbor, Hawaii. The facility had been hurriedly built during World War II to take in wounded soldiers and sailors from the Pacific. My father had enlisted amid the country's patriotic fervor at the end of the war, after failing to find his academic footing during a single semester at Creighton University, where he planned to study pharmacy. By the time he joined up in January 1946, the war was over and the Hawaiian hospital where he worked was about as lively as a tomb. He was bored to death and anxious to finish his military duty so he could return to Omaha and marry his South High School sweetheart, Helen Marie Strack.

His pining for Helen and frustrations over Navy tedium are palpable in the letters. He was in an unusually sour mood, yet he found it in his heart to express touching kindness, once again, when his mother wrote that she was planning to remarry. *"Mom, you know I could never be mad at you for marrying again,"* he wrote from Hawaii in 1947. *"Mom, as long as you are happy, I am glad. You deserve all of the happiness in the world, mom."* I was stopped cold by one other bit of proof of Eddie's extraordinary solicitousness toward Hazel. Her little suitcase contained a Western Union telegram, sent from Omaha to Michigan at 5:57 p.m. on June 17, 1949, the evening before my father married my mother. It read, *"DEAR MOM: YOUR WEDDING INVITATION RETURNED SENT TO WRONG ADDRESS WIRING TO LET YOU KNOW WE DIDN'T FORGET YOU LOVE=HELEN AND EDDIE="*

My father was no pushover. He was a tough, intelligent, and determined man. Yet somehow, in spite of a life story filled with hurt and tragedy, he exuded an essential sweetness that is manifest in these letters. Rereading his messages to his mother from Hawaii, I decided that if my father could be so kind and respectful toward the mother who had betrayed him to the bone, I owed it to both of them to try to better understand Hazel's journey through life. Everyone deserves to have their story properly told, even a loathsome mother. As a writer, I know that you can't really fully profile a person until you've done diligent research. But I knew almost nothing about my grandmother, having met her just twice during her rare visits to Nebraska. Most of what I knew was second- or thirdhand. So I began snooping around. As expected, I quickly discovered that the family lore does not necessarily align with the facts that I was able to exhume about Hazel and her family. So before we get to the letters, let me tell you what I found out about my runaway grandmother and her people. It was quite a family.

South Omaha Girl

HAZEL LEE CHANDLER WAS BORN in South Omaha, the third daughter of itinerant parents with shallow roots in Texas and Kansas. She was the runt of a family that was on the rangy side. Like her older sisters, she was bestowed by her parents, Grace Taylor and William Bazell Chandler, with a name drawn from nature. Grace gave birth to four of Bill Chandler's children: Agnes Daisy in 1902; Cecilia Leafy in 1904; a brother in 1907, and Hazel Lee about 18 months later, on September 4, 1908. The Chandler girls were known by the Mother Earthy names of Daisy, Leafy, and Hazel. Grace also had an outdoorsy pet name for her youngest daughter: She called Hazel "Hootie." But this naming creativity stopped with the girls. Their brother was not Elwood or Florian or Oakley — not even Woody. He was named John, after Grace's father.

The girls had personalities as vivid as their names. "These ladies were all a piece of work," Janean Nelson Haukap, Daisy's granddaughter, told me. Daisy was the beauty of the family, with an olive complexion, piercing dark eyes, and a model's smile. Leafy and John shared their own striking feature. Their powder-blue

Daisy Chandler, circa 1920

eyes, inherited from their father, seemed to gleam like white alabaster. Leafy's blue eyes were a signature trait into adulthood. Each of the girls was also blessed with thick, wavy hair that a little humidity would tighten into stylish curls. My stepmother, Beverly Krajicek, met Hazel several times in the 1970s. Four decades later, she still remembered her coif. "Hazel had the most wonderful head of hair you can imagine," Beverly told me. "It was thick with a lovely curl. Anyone in the world would want that head of hair." Robert Haukap, Janean's husband, told me that whatever attractiveness the Chandler girls had, it must have come from the father's side. Bob and Janean live in rural Iowa, near where Daisy spent the last half of her life after a raucous start in South Omaha that landed her name in newspaper crime stories several times. Haukap, a family historian, says his research suggests no tendency toward attractiveness among Grace Taylor's branch of the family. "The Taylor women were all homely," Haukap told me.

Booming Cowtowns

Although she was just 21 years old at the time, Grace Taylor's marriage to Bill Chandler was her second. She brought a 4-year-old son into the relationship when she and Bill were wed in 1901 in Grace's hometown of Wichita, Kansas. At age 28, Bill Chandler had seven years on his new bride. He, too, had been around the corral a time or two. According to his family's oral history, Chandler married young and fathered a son, named Dean Chandler. Confirmation of that marriage does not show up in official records, but Bill Chandler decades later would tell a federal Census-taker that he was 18 years old at the time of his first marriage. Bob Haukap says that make-believe marriages and divorces were a family tradition among the Chandlers and Taylors. "I think it must have been a way of life for them back then," he told me. "It seems like they didn't always marry when they said they did. And when they did marry, they didn't always divorce."

   This much I know for sure: Bill Chandler was born in 1873 in Belton, Texas, the second of four children of Daniel and Tabitha Chandler. The family had just arrived in Belton, which was then a dusty dot on the state's central frontier halfway between Austin and Waco. U.S. Census records show that Bill's father, the son of an Illinois farmer, worked in Texas as a railroad laborer. Daniel and Tabitha grew up and were married in Fayette County, in central Illinois. (They spent their early years together in Flora, Illinois, an interesting coincidence considering the floral names later given their son's three daughters.) Daniel Chandler and his wife and children moved frequently, which suggests financial instability. Perhaps he was following railroad work. Census records show that the Chandlers pulled up stakes every few years and moved—west from Illinois to Atlantic, Iowa, back to Illinois, down to Texas, and finally to Omaha, where Daniel died young in 1885, just before his 40th birthday.

Bill Chandler was 12 when his father died. By his teen years, he was splitting time between Wichita and Omaha, booming cowtowns 300 miles apart. Each city saw its population explode after the founding of their Union Stockyards, in 1883 in Omaha and four years later in Wichita. Omaha's population increased from 30,000 in 1880 to 140,000 ten years later. Meatpacking plants and related factories sprouted like mushrooms around the Stockyards, attracting thousands of American migrants and European immigrants, including my Krajicek ancestors from Bohemia. Wichita was (and is) a much smaller city, but its stockyards prompted a similar boom on a smaller scale. Its population rose fivefold to 25,000 between 1880 and 1890.

With labor in demand, streams of Europeans—from Poland, Germany, Ireland, Italy, Bohemia, Croatia, Lithuania, and many others—journeyed over the ocean to make a new start in middle America. That is the Krajicek immigrant story. But the Chandler and Taylor ancestors, Americans for many generations dating to the early 1800s, had long and winding roads of their own. As the American interior opened for settlement, the Taylors and Chandlers funneled toward Nebraska and Kansas from places like Kentucky, North Carolina, and Virginia. Some wandered for years before reaching a final destination, with stops in Illinois, Missouri, and

Iowa. The Chandler-Taylor branch is heavy with ancestral stock from the United Kingdom. An analysis of my DNA shows that my blood relatives were big-city dwellers, having lived in places such as London and Liverpool, England; Glasgow and Edinburgh, Scotland, and Dublin, Ireland. Some of that blood flowed to me via grandmother Hazel.

Big O & Doo-Dah

Ancestors of Grace Taylor, Hazel's mother, were very early arrivals on the American shores. The astonishingly detailed records compiled by the Mormon Church show that Grace's great-great-grandfather, Rawleigh Alexander Taylor, was born in Virginia in 1763, 13 years before America declared independence. Rawleigh's wife, Elizabeth Waddell, was the daughter of an immigrant from Glasgow, Scotland. Mormon genealogical records trace the Waddell family tree in Scotland back to 1470.

More than 400 years later, their descendants in America were ping-ponging between the two midcontinent cities that would become affectionately known as the Big O (Omaha) and Doo-Dah (Wichita). Grace's parents, John Taylor and Edith Butler, spent time in Iowa and Missouri before arriving in Wichita in about 1877, just before the city's boom. Grace was born there on September 5, 1880, the fifth of seven children. Records show that on August 6, 1896, a month before her 16th birthday, Grace married a man named Charles Brown in Kansas City, Kansas. A son, Bert Brown, was born 16 months later, in December 1897. The marriage did not last, and Grace soon returned to her family. According to family lore, Bert Brown had black features and was presumed to be of mixed race. A photo passed along by a relative shows Bert with a broad nose and thick lips, but Hazel, his half-sister, shared those same traits, and both of her parents were as white as rice. Kansas was among the relatively few places in the United States that allowed interracial marriage in the 1890s, so it is possible that Grace Taylor's first husband was a Black man. That would not have been allowed in Nebraska, where its racist "anti-miscegenation" law was intact until 1963.

By 1900, the Taylor family had moved from Wichita to South Omaha, where father John worked as a packinghouse laborer. The 1900 Census showed that John, Edith and all seven of their children—with ages spanning from 27 to 13— were living together at 2801 V Street, in a neighborhood of rickety houses in the meatpacking district that was later demolished to make way for Omaha's largest housing project, Southside Terrace. The Taylors lived close enough to hear the baying cattle in the Omaha Stockyards—and the bellows of drunks stumbling home from the gritty bars that overserved meatpackers. Like their father, two of Grace's older brothers also worked in that trade. Census documents identified Grace as single, not divorced, and her son, Bert, was not included in the household roster. Perhaps it was an oversight; perhaps the boy was with his father in Kansas City.

It was a short walk from the Taylor home to any of the hulking, red brick factories of the Big Five firms—Armour, Swift, Wilson, Cudahy, and Morris—that had nationalized meat production in America. Inside, workers slaughtered, butchered, packaged, and distributed cattle, hogs, and lambs brought to market at the Stockyards. The livestock yards and packinghouses defined South Omaha for generations, from the 1880s to the 1960s. And the balance of Grace Taylor's life would be lived out within sniffing distance of the manure that doomed animals emitted on their final walk to slaughter. That was South Omaha—blood and toil, stinky and sweaty. Once a separate town, it had a population of 40,000 when it was annexed by Omaha in 1915. There are no mansions in South O. It is one of those working-class towns with broad shoulders, to borrow Carl Sandburg's famous description of Chicago.

South Omaha was and is a blue-collar place whose lifeblood flows from an ever-changing stream of immigrants — once from Europe, now from Latin America and the Sudan. The founders made it easy for newcomers to navigate. There are none of the winding boulevards or broad avenues that you find in wealthier sections of Omaha; clearly, South Omaha was designed by a draftsman's ruler, not an artist's brush. That quadrant of the city is laid out in a sensible grid between the Missouri River to the east, 72nd Street to the west, Vinton and Grover Streets to the north, and Harrison Street to the south. Even the street names are user-friendly — ascending numbers from east to west, the ascending alphabet and a handful of presidents' names from north to south. Many neighborhoods were Balkanized by ethnicity, with Catholic churches as home base for each nationality — St. Stanislaus for the Polish, St. Anthony's for Lithuanians, Sts. Peter and Paul for Croatians, Assumption for Czechs, and so forth.

In the meatpacking district, thousands of new arrivals lived clustered in warrens of tiny houses that pressed in tight around the packinghouses. They were beckoned to work by screaming steam whistles that roused them from bed six mornings a week and blew periodic blasts as clock-in time approached. It was physically demanding, assembly-line work — on your feet, repeating the same task over and over until the whistle blew at day's end. Many laborers then retreated to the beer joints that lined Q Street, the main drag of the meatpacking district. One day long ago in my boyhood, I overheard my saucy maternal grandmother, Eileen Strack, rant about the rowdy bars. "South Omaha has three bars for every church," said my grandma, who lived just off Q Street, "and it's got a church on pert-near every damned corner!"

The Q Street saloons catered to two distinct clienteles. Thirsty out-of-town farmers and ranchers toted heavy wallets into the barrooms after bringing their livestock to market. They sat on barstools beside the blood-stained, accented immigrants who earned a living in the packinghouses as boners, scullers, and luggers of that same livestock. Either occupation was a rough way to make a buck, and South Omaha was teeming with swindlers and cons scheming to get a hand in their pocket.

A Broken Family

The crooked paths of Grace Taylor and Bill Chandler crossed in unruly South O as the new century began. Family lore suggests that young Bill Chandler was an outlaw—perhaps a bootlegger. If so, he might have started a family tradition. I discovered in my research that Chandler's eldest daughter, the ever-fascinating Daisy, was arrested in a federal moonshining raid in Omaha in the 1930s. Bill Chandler traveled frequently between Wichita and Omaha, both wide open towns where anyone who knew where to look could scratch an itch for all the vices, major and minor. Census records say Chandler worked as a stockyards yardman while in Omaha and as supervisor of a concrete paving crew while in Wichita, although that's not to say that he didn't maintain a felonious side job.

Grace and Bill returned to Kansas to marry and begin their life together. Records show they were wed in Wichita in 1901. The 1910 U.S. Census found the family living in a rented house at 2201 E. 13th Street in that city's North Central section. The house was packed to the rafters. There were Bill and Grace and their four kids, ages 8, 6, 3, and 2. Census-taker James Miller found three others living with them when he visited on April 18, 1910. They included Bert Brown, 13, Grace's son from her Kansas City marriage, and two adult boarders, Edward Winn, 45, and Louis McDowell, 22. Census documents say the boarders were concrete laborers—presumably from Bill's crew.

A charming photo shot in about that same year shows the Chandler kids in ragamuffin cuteness. They were gathered on a porch,

Chandler Children, Wichita, Kansas, circa 1910

likely at the same Wichita house. Raven-haired Hazel, looking stern, is seated on the lap of Daisy, who is wearing comically oversized second-hand shoes. Little John, leaning in from the left, is barefoot and wears another hand-me-down: a dark dress with a dainty lace collar. Leafy, with the striking blue eyes, cozies up from the right. The children's broad personalities shine through, even at early ages.

The Chandlers had moved from Wichita back to Nebraska by 1914. Records show that Daisy, at age 12, was Baptized that year at

David J. Krajicek

St. Agnes Catholic Church, at South 23rd and Q Streets in South Omaha. Hazel and her brother, John, were Baptized together at St. Agnes in November 1920, as adolescents.

On January 10, 1920, a U.S. Census enumerator found the Chandler family intact and living together in a rented house at 5220 S. 24th St., at the edge of South Omaha's main shopping district, just south of Q Street along a stretch of buildings demolished long ago. Father Bill was working at the Stockyards. A formal posed photograph from that era features the parents and four children, as well as full-grown Bert Brown and Dean Chandler, the sons from Bill and Grace's earlier relationships.

It's a handsome family portrait, although the mustachioed father seems burdened or distracted. Perhaps Bill Chandler had leaving on his mind. Within a year, his marriage to Grace was over. Both

The Chandler Family: (from left) John, Daisy, Dean, father William, Bert Brown, mother Grace, Leafy, and Hazel, Omaha, circa 1918

partners moved on quickly. Grace married for a third time on January 7, 1921, just a year after the Census visit. The ceremony was held across the Missouri River from Omaha in Council Bluffs, Iowa. Records show that her new spouse was a man named John Harry Wilson. He was 37 years old, four years younger than his bride. Wilson was born in Chicago in about 1883. Like Grace's first marriage—as a teenager to Charles Brown in Kansas City—the third was finished not long after it started. Wilson was out of her life by 1930—whether dead or simply gone, I'm not sure.

In the meantime, Bill Chandler had abandoned Omaha and wandered south through Kansas to Oklahoma. It was there on November 28, 1922, that he tied the knot—or the slipknot—once again. His new wife was Lucretia Hogan, a divorced Kansas native. At age 39, she was eight years younger than Bill. Lucretia apparently was childless, but Bill Chandler fixed that. She gave birth to a daughter, Billie, in 1926. Four years later, a 1930 a federal Census-taker found the couple and 4-year-old Billie living together in a small house in the oil fields east of Oklahoma City. Chandler had found a new career as a building contractor, according to the Census.

Ed Krajicek and his sister Anna, South Omaha, circa 1935

Hazel and Ed

HAZEL WAS ABOUT 13 YEARS OLD, in the midst of adolescence, when her parents split up. That surely was a burden for Grace and her children—financially, emotionally, and socially. The Mormon Church's vast initiative to digitalize Census tracts, marriage and death records, and detailed family trees gives researchers like me quick access to an unprecedented depth of genealogical information. This is fleshed out—sometimes accurately, sometimes not—with oral histories and family lore. But even with all this material, cobbling together a complete story of the lives of Edward F. Krajicek and Hazel Lee Chandler is like to trying to put together a 1,000-piece puzzle that is missing half its pieces. We can see the edges and contours of their lives, but the big picture is gauzy. We can, however, make some assumptions based on common sense.

Modern family counselors stress the importance of parents as role models to show their offspring how to create healthy intimate relationships. Let's assume that Grace and Bill Chandler and the rugged, unrefined denizens of the South Omaha meatpacking district were not always exemplars of polite social niceties.

Hazel adored her sister Daisy. But Daisy was a wild child who attracted men like bees to pollen. Hazel was also close with her Aunt Minnie Taylor Ford, Grace's sister. Minnie was married to James Ford, a packinghouse butcher. Later in life, Minnie was a South Omaha card sharp, and she dressed the part in celluloid eyeshade while running a regular game out of a boarding house she operated near 24th and L Streets.

Marygrace Chandler Hansen, daughter of John Chandler, is the last living offspring of the four Chandler siblings. Marygrace, who grew up in the Upland Park neighborhood of South Omaha, did not know her father well and has been conducting her own investigation of the Chandler family, much of which she generously shared with me. Marygrace says she recalls visiting Aunt Minnie's home in the mid-1960s. "Minnie Ford had a rooming house behind the South Omaha Post Office," Marygrace told me. "My mom and me would go over to the house, and she was always playing cards, wearing her green visor." Minnie was more interested in her card game than making nice with her visiting niece. "She was not very accommodating," Marygrace said, "but I wandered about looking at old family pictures hanging from the walls." The origin of Ed and Hazel's love story is one of the missing pieces of the family puzzle, but a genealogical detail unearthed by Marygrace offers a hint. Card sharp Minnie may have played a role in their meeting.

Immigrant Struggles

Edward F. Krajicek also came from a broken family, fractured not by divorce but by the tragic death of the paterfamilias. His father, Vaclav Krajicek, had emigrated in about 1890 from rural Bohemia, where his family had farmed for many generations. As the third-born son, Vaclav had no chance of inheriting the family farm, so he followed a cousin's path over the ocean to Omaha. He settled in the Bohemian enclave near 13th and William Streets, just south of downtown, and labored amid the toxic environment of a lead smeltery. He was often laid off during slow times and was forced to scramble to find other forms of manual labor to fill those gaps.

In 1897, Vaclav, 27, married Anna Kopecky, 20, a fellow Bohemian who had emigrated with her parents as a teenager. (They had grown up in villages 25 miles apart.) Vaclav and Anna produced a bounty of offspring — six children born over 10 years, beginning with Anna in 1899, James in 1901, and Edward Francis, my grandfather, in 1903. In 1904, Vaclav quit the smeltery and rented a farm in the fertile rolling hills at Omaha's western edge, near what is now 84th and Q Streets. Vaclav and Anna raised livestock and farm crops, and their operation earned a profit, even as they were hampered by drought in their first three years on the farm, according to an account written decades later by their son James.

Meanwhile, the babies kept coming — Frank, known as Darby, in 1905, and Rose in 1908. Two years later, in the spring of 1910, Vaclav was diagnosed with Bright's Disease, an inflammation of the kidneys. Anna, pregnant with their sixth child, drove Vaclav by wagon to a hospital in Omaha, where doctors said there was no hope. She took him home to die. On June 28, 1910, their last child, Godfrey (known as Red) was born. But any joy was muted. Vaclav died 109 days later, on October 15, 1910. He was 40 years old and had spent exactly half his lifetime in America. He left a 33-year-old widow and six children, ages 11, 9, 7, 5, 2 and four months. Anna and her kids harvested a final crop with the help of a Krajicek cousin who farmed adjacent property. According to family lore, Anna sold the livestock, grain, and farm machinery, then used the proceeds to buy a four-room house that was moved on skids to a lot she purchased at 5707 S. 36th Street. Her parents and other kin lived nearby, in the tiny shotgun shacks of an immigrant ghetto known as Goose Hollow. Anna's house was eventually expanded to accommodate the six children, and life went on relatively smoothly, according to the lore.

But in researching this history, I was surprised to learn that life without Vaclav included a traumatic detour that had been erased from the Krajicek narrative. I found the fatherless family in the 1920 Census, but they were not living in the little house on South 36th Street. Instead, nine years after the death of Vaclav, Anna and her kids were living as lodgers in a downtown Omaha tenement building at 8th and Dodge Streets, at edge of the industrial hive known as Jobbers Canyon. Census documents show that their building was filled with the indigent and unemployed, many of them recent immigrants. The federal welfare system wasn't created until 1935, 15 years later, but perhaps the tenement's poor occupants were subsidized by the city or religious charities. Unfortunately, Census data does not reveal how long the Krajiceks had been living there. It could have been a temporary measure during renovation of their house.

Despite their humble circumstances, the Krajiceks were not idle in 1920. The Census shows that half the family was working in packinghouses—mother Anna, 43, as a pork trimmer; daughter Anna, 21, as a clerk; James, 18, as a hog sculler, and Edward, 16, as a carpenter in the box factory, assembly crates used to ship beef by railroad. The three youngest were still in school: Darby, 14, Rose, 12, and Red, 9. In a letter written in the 1960s to a Czech relative, James Krajicek recalled that the family's tight finances required his mother to work in a packinghouse for 10 years. He said he and his siblings quit school to help free Anna from the factory. As James wrote in his letter, "In 1921, when the three oldest children were working, we thought that mother should not have to work any longer. From that time until her death, mother remained at the home."

As a writer, I've always been interested in collecting our family's stories, and I enjoyed asking Grandpa Krajicek about his life. He had quit school after sixth grade, still an adolescent. He regretted his lack of education, but he told me during conversations in the '80s and '90s that he and his siblings could not bear to have their mother laboring in the packinghouse. It shamed them.

My grandfather was a simple man, but he was as reliable as the sunrise. He worked the same job for 49 years, from 1916 to 1965. He was employed by the Cudahy Packing Company, one of the meat industry's Big Five, but he rarely touched meat. He had a specialty position, swinging an oversized hatchet-style hammer to build beef shipping crates. He was proud of his job. "Good clean work," he would tell me, compared to those who wore smocks stained with animal blood on the killing floors and butcher lines. Ed was an unusually tall man for his generation, and his right fist was like a steel cudgel from endless hours of wielding his hatchet. As a young man, he spent many weekend nights earning a few drinks as a bouncer in the tough meatpacking district saloons. He didn't lose many fights. As he liked to growl, "I had more power in my right arm than most men had in their entire bodies."

Council Bluffs Quickies

Grandpa sometimes mentioned Hazel in our conversations, usually to warn me against dating girls of Irish ancestry. But he would get a gleam in his eye when he talked about "the old cat," as he called her. I think he still had a thing for her, 50 years after she dumped him. I didn't have the good sense to ask him how they met. For more than five years, Marygrace Hansen and I have exchanged phone calls, emails, documents, and photographs about our parallel family research. Her father, John Chandler, led a troubled life that included serious psychiatric and alcohol issues—the latter an affliction for his sisters Hazel and Daisy, as well. One day, Marygrace sent a note to let me know that my grandfather's name had shown up on a marriage certificate that she had come across. The South Omaha wedding was between a man named Fred Beck and Fern Ford, Minnie (the gambler) Taylor Ford's daughter. Minnie was Hazel's aunt, and the two families were very close; the Chandlers and Fords lived next door to each other at 24th and Q in 1920.

Ed Krajicek was an official witness to Fern and Fred's wedding, on June 26, 1926. Obviously, he was a close friend of the groom. And it seems logical that Daisy, Leafy, and Hazel would have attended the wedding celebration of their first cousin, Fern. Is this where Ed and Hazel set eyes on one another? Hazel, buxom and sturdily built, would have been a nubile young woman, 10 weeks short of her 18th birthday. And Ed certainly was an eligible bachelor. As he approached his 23rd birthday, he was still living with his mother and several siblings on South 36th Street. He was a reliable workman, with nearly a decade of flawless attendance at Cudahy. And while he wasn't exactly Clark Gable with his round, Slavic face, his height gave him a commanding physical presence.

If they did meet and began dating at that June wedding, they enjoyed a long courtship. Hazel and Ed were married 16 months later, on October 19, 1927. He was 24, and she was 19. A couple of things struck me when I studied the scant details of their ceremony. They were married on a Wednesday. That seemed odd. And they traveled across the Missouri River to Council Bluffs, Iowa, for a ceremony in a government clerk's office, just as Hazel's mother had when she remarried in 1921.

Iowa had no marital waiting period, so Council Bluffs in the 1920s functioned as Las Vegas for hot-to-trot Nebraskans. (In 1931, Iowa legislators passed a "gin marriage law" that mandated a five-day wait to deter drunken unions.) The Chandler family apparently was quite schooled in the ins and outs of quickie marriages. Hazel's cache of letters included one sent by her sister Leafy from Kansas City in 1946. It included an amusing tangent about Daisy's oldest daughter, Grace. Leafy wrote, *'I think Grace is going to get married. She called the other night from Westside [a town in Iowa] and told me not to tell Daisy. She wanted to know if they had to wait three days here in K.C. I asked her who the boy was but she wouldn't tell me. I haven't heard any more. I told her you do have to wait here in Missouri but not in Kansas."*

So did Ed and Hazel cross the river to Iowa on a Wednesday because they were in a hurry? The first of their two sons, my father, Eddie, was born on July 2, 1928. That was 256 days after they married—24 days short of the (admittedly flexible) "normal" pregnancy term of 280 days. Maybe their first child was a honeymoon baby who arrived early. But maybe not. He was named Edward Lee, sharing his father's first name and his mother's middle name. He began life in an upstairs apartment at 2414 L Street, a few steps from the bustling crossroads of 24th and L. The couple's second son, Conrad Jerome, arrived 16 months along, on October 26, 1929. Three days after Connie's birth, the Stock Market Crash of 1929 touched off the Great Depression. My research found the young family living the following April at a new address eight blocks away—with Hazel's mother. I suspect the crashing economy was a factor in the move.

South 23rd Street

Somehow, Grace Chandler had landed on her feet by 1930, a decade after her husband Bill ran off and left her with four kids. On April 13 that year, a Census enumerator named Ethel C. Berry climbed the steps to a tiny single-family house at 5417 S. 23rd St., a few blocks up the hill from low-lying Brown Park. She found the house occupied by Grace Chandler, daughter Hazel, son-in-law Ed Krajicek and two grandsons, Eddie and Connie, ages 21 months and six months. Grace told Berry that she owned the house, which she valued at $3,500—roughly the equivalent of $55,000 in 2020. Chandler told the Census-taker that she was a widow. Bill Chandler was alive and living in Oklahoma. Perhaps she was referring to her 1921 marriage to John Harry Wilson in Council Bluffs, who by vague family lore may have died of cancer.

Grace's little house became a hub for her daughters and grandchildren. Built in 1918, it sits about 10 feet above street level and is tucked onto a lot that covers just one-seventh of an acre—6,500 square feet. To this day, its predominant feature is a miniscule flat-top concrete block garage sunk into the sloping bank at street level. That is where the Krajicek-Chandler union began to mature—or fester—with three adults and two growing boys crammed together.

When they reached school age, Eddie and Connie attended St. Agnes, the Catholic elementary school (now demolished) at 23rd and Q Streets, a block from Grace's house. Ed would have been out of the house early every day, hoofing it about a mile each way to the sprawling Cudahy factory near 36th and O Streets. After work, he developed habit of stopping on Q Street for a couple of draft beers and a shot of whiskey. As I've noted, Hazel's drinking (and accompanying moral turpitude) ruined the marriage, according to the family's conventional wisdom. Both Ed and Hazel had a robust thirst, but he managed to maintain control. The arc of Hazel's life demonstrates that she did not—and clearly was not cut out for motherhood. On the other hand, I am a descendant of the fruit of that union, so who am I to say it was a bad idea? Ed Krajicek could be gruff, and Hazel was no shrinking violet. The two went at it from time to time. My Grandpa was hard of hearing from a young age. According to a family story, Hazel conked Ed on the head with a lamp during a set-to, and Grandpa Krajicek believed that blow was the genesis of his poor hearing.

When I began looking into the Krajicek-Chandler story, I assumed that the marriage began well enough then faded, like so many. Officially, it lasted about nine years, from 1927 until Hazel left in 1936. But while scouring Omaha newspaper archives for clues, I was surprised to discover that serious conflict had begun much earlier. In June 1930, just nine months after Connie was born, Ed Krajicek filed a petition for divorce from Hazel. An agate-type listing in the Omaha *World-Herald* noted the grounds: cruelty. Ed did not follow through, and they stayed together for another six years. But the court filing is black-and-white evidence that the marriage was troubled from the start. Sadly, as a grown man my father revealed to loved ones that, as a first-grader, he once came home from school to find his mother in a love clutch with a stranger. I'm not sure that the lurid details matter all these decades later. Let's just agree that they were a moral mismatch. As my stepmother, Beverly, put it, "I think your Grandpa and Hazel were two people who should have never gotten married."

As I will explain later, Hazel's move to Michigan did not fill the hole in her gullet — or her soul. Her step-kin there told me recently that her addiction to alcohol only deepened as she grew older. As one relative who knew her well told me, "She always carried a pint in her apron pocket." She said Hazel could be a mean drunk who often dissolved into morose weeping. We shouldn't be surprised, based on Hazel's reputation in Omaha. But it was nonetheless distressing to confirm that my grandmother's primary committed relationship was with Kessler whiskey.

I do want to dispel one often-repeated family myth: that the Chandler family had Native American blood. One of my father's cousins told me that her wing of the family had always believed Hazel, with her dark hair and olive skin, couldn't control her drinking because she was part Indian — the cliché disparagement of native people. Likewise, I learned that her Michigan kin also seemed to believe that she was part Cherokee. But it's not true. Neither Hazel nor her parents had Indian ancestors. I know this with certainty because my DNA shows absolutely no Native American lineage, which would have been passed down to me from my grandparents and great-grandparents. I assumed the confusion arose because Bill Chandler supposedly married a native woman, Lucretia Hogan, after leaving Grace. But I checked that out, too. Lucretia's parents, William and Abigail Hogan, were farmers. He was originally from Indiana, she from Kentucky. Both Lucretia and her parents identified themselves as white, not Indian, on every U.S. Census I could find, from as early as 1870 to as late as 1940. I don't know where the Indian myth came from, but I'm certain that the Krajicek-Chandler line can't use that tired old excuse to explain any failings with alcohol — and we had plenty of them.

Bootlegging & Bloodshed

TO FURTHER EXAMINE THE CHANDLERS, we need to take a side trip down one more South Omaha back alley to consider the life that Daisy Chandler led there. Daisy was the queen bee among her siblings, and to understand Hazel you need to know a bit more about her oldest sister.

While she was long on looks, Daisy was short on judgment. She certainly stumbled out of the starting gate of romance. On March 1, 1921, two months after her mother's third marriage to the mysterious Mr. Wilson, Daisy followed Grace's path across the river for another of the Chandler family's midweek Council Bluffs weddings. Her groom was Frederick Johan Rupp, known as Fritzie. The bride and groom were both about 19 years old—going on 13. Neither one seemed to have much sense.

Rupp, tall and husky, was a sketchy figure who came from German immigrant stock. "By all accounts, Fritzie was a two-bit South Omaha hoodlum," Bob Haukup, the Chandler family historian, told me. "He'd hang around the Stockyards and steal anything he could get his hands on, like piglets, which he would then turn

around and sell. He'd get a wad of cash and disappear. The story is
that he was gone more often than not—went out for cigarettes and
disappeared for months or years, that sort of thing." He was
around long enough to father a child, Grace Rupp, whose birth was
announced in *World-Herald* agate type on October 14, 1921, seven
and a half months after mom and dad's Council Bluffs wedding.
Flighty Fritzie was gone before his daughter took her first steps.
Daisy, striking even with an infant on her hip, was running a café
near the Stockyards, where men flocked to her like butterflies to
zinnias. One of her suitors was a meat salesman, Raymond Aldo
Ford, who called on the cafe. With Fritzie on the hoof, Daisy embarked on a prolonged dalliance with Ford that led to another pregnancy and a second daughter, Jean, born in 1924.

Ford and Daisy apparently were married briefly because
Haukap unearthed a copy of their divorce decree, on the grounds
of lack of support. Daisy and Fritzie Rupp may have then remarried—if, in fact, they bothered with a divorce after their first go-
around. Chandler family lore says the couple was married twice.
But as Bob Haukap noted, they had a habit of claiming make-believe marriages and divorces. Whether they were remarried or not,
my research shows that Fritzie Rupp returned to Omaha—and to
Daisy's bosom—by 1930.

He ought to have stayed away, as things turned out.

Rupp was easy to track because his name had a habit of show-
ing up in newspaper stories. In January 1931, he was ticketed after
a serious auto accident in which Fritzie rear-ended a car, injuring
a child in the back seat when his truck pushed that vehicle into a
bridge abutment. Five months later, he was back in the news
when he was hurt by a 200-pound cake of ice that fell on him in
the icehouse at Swift & Co. packinghouse, were he was working.
The most interesting thing about that story was Rupp's address:

5417 S. 23rd Street, Grace Chandler's tiny house, which was also occupied then by Ed and Hazel and their boys. If Fritzie was living there, it stands to reason that so was Daisy and her daughters—a total of five adults and four children.

On October 20, 1933, the *World-Herald* noted that Daisy had filed for divorce against Rupp. (For their first marriage or the alleged second? It's hard to say.) But even then, Daisy couldn't quit him. Two years later, in March 1935, Daisy and Fritzie were living together at 5251 S. 24th Street, near Q. Twice that month, both Fritzie and Daisy's names made the newspapers. On March 9, Rupp was arrested and fined $15 for receiving stolen property. Police reported that Fritzie bought a stack of 10 packs of playing cards from an 11-year-old boy. The kid had shoplifted the cards from Woolworth's Five & Dime on South 24th Street. Before he was bundled away to juvenile detention, the boy saved Fritzie from jail time by lying that Rupp did not know that cards were stolen. The caper earned the delinquent boy a buck —10 cents a pack.

Six days later, it was Daisy's turn for a spotlight and handcuffs. On March 15, 1935, local police and federal agents raided her home as part of a national roundup of "counterfeiters, dopers, and moonshiners," as a *World-Herald* headline put it. Daisy was charged with possession of 22 gallons of homemade hooch. Prohibition had finally ended in Nebraska in 1934, but selling homebrew was a federal felony for tax evasion. Bob Haukap told me Chandler lore suggests that Daisy had been selling moonshine out the backdoor of her Stockyards café for years. She has indicted by a federal grand jury, almost certainly based on the testimony of an unnamed informant who bought her liquor then ratted her out. She pleaded innocent, but that case was destined to be overshadowed by more deadly events that followed just months later.

The Clothesline War

As 1935 drew to a close, the Chandler girls were living within shouting distance of one another at the edge of downtown South Omaha. Hazel was with her mother, husband, and boys on South 23rd. Daisy, Fritzie and the two girls were about a block away, at 5251 South 24th. And Leafy was right next door to Daisy, at 5255 South 24th, with her husband, salesman Emmett Eggleston, and two young sons, Bob and Jack. Family proximity can bring comfort—and conflict. Early on New Year's morning 1936, a petty disagreement over a clothesline, of all things, touched off a squabble that escalated into a seminal event in Chandler family history. It all landed Fritzie Rupp's name in the newspapers one last time.

Daisy and Fritzie partied late that New Year's Eve, arriving home long after the last refrain of Auld Lang Syne. At 4:30 a.m., Daisy saw a light burning next door and went over to wish Leafy a happy new year. As the *World-Herald* reported, "Fred, who had been drinking,...followed her into the Eggleston home. Because of ill feeling between the two brothers-in-law, Eggleston ordered Rupp from the house."

Daisy and Fritzie retreated to their own home, but Leafy knew her sister wouldn't be safe. It was no secret in the family that Fritzie frequently assaulted his wife. "He'll be beating her up," Leafy told Eggleston after the brouhaha. Standing at a window with a cocked ear, she heard screams and rushed next door to find Fritzie wailing on Daisy. When Leafy tried to intercede, "Rupp then turned upon her, knocking her down, tearing her clothes from her, and kicking her," according to a prosecutor's account quoted in the newspaper. Leafy broke away and fled home, with Fritzie in close pursuit. Emmett Eggleston waited at the back door, armed with a butcher knife. When Rupp approached, Emmett raised the knife toward his brother-in-law's throat, and an artery was soon spurting blood. As Fritzie was hemorrhaging profusely, the sisters and Eggleston carried Rupp across the yard and back home, leaving a crimson trail.

Police finally were summoned and rushed Fritzie to a hospital, but the wound was fatal.

Just a day later, Daisy, Leafy, and Emmett sat before a coroner's inquest and testified that Fritzie was a violent bully who often slapped and assaulted both women. They explained that Rupp's relationship with Eggleston had deteriorated the previous summer in a crazy dispute over the clothesline in the Rupps' backyard. Daisy offered to share the line with her sister, but Fritzie tore Leafy's clothes down and stomped them into the dirt. When Emmett confronted Fritzie about his strange actions, the much larger Rupp assaulted him. Eggleston told the coroner's jury that he had lived "in terror" of Rupp ever since. Emmett testified that he did not intend to slash Rupp—that his brother-in-law ran into the raised butcher knife. The coroner's jury bought his version. According the *World-Herald*, the inquest "completely exonerated the small, plump Emmett Eggleston . . . from blame for killing his towering brother-in-law."

The homicide was a breaking point for the Egglestons, who soon moved three hours south to Kansas City. They had had enough of South O. This created a dilemma for the couple. Hazel had asked Leafy and Emmett to be Eddie's godparents. They stood at his Baptism in July 1928 and vowed to uphold their Catholic obligation to serve as his proxy parents should Ed and Hazel become unable. Hazel's abandonment later in 1936 made those vows highly pertinent. To their credit, Leafy and Emmett went out of their way to maintain lifelong relationships with both Eddie and Connie, even via long distance.

Daisy got out of South Omaha, too. She found a new man, James Gilroy Lidgett, and by the spring of 1946 they were living together as husband and wife on a farm in Vail, Iowa, where Daisy operated another café. She didn't like to share much about her wild younger days, according to Bob Haukap. "Daisy and her oldest daughter, Grace Rupp Lindberg, were very protective and deceitful about

their past life in South Omaha," Haukap told me. He had re-
searched his own family tree, and he began to do the same with his
wife's Chandler branch. "Aunt Grace was silently furious," he said,
"and always resented me for it."

* * *

Eddie Krajicek was just 7 years old when his Uncle Emmett killed
his Uncle Fritzie, but he surely would have been aware of this cata-
strophic event among relatives living so close. As an adult, he
sometimes shared vignettes about the irrepressible Chandlers with
his wife, Beverly. These stories left her with an unmistakable feeling about them. "In my opinion, that family was riffraff," she told
me. "That doesn't mean they were dumb riffraff, but they were def-
initely riffraff."

Onward to Michigan

I haven't identified any particular precipitating event that pushed
Hazel out the door in 1936. She and Ed apparently had managed to
patch over whatever conflict prompted him to file for divorce in
1930. Perhaps the Fritzie Rupp slaying somehow played a role in
her decision to leave. If my family's lore is sound, she left of her
own volition and Ed, still living with Hazel's mother, gave her a
chance to reconsider.

"I don't know if it was the first time she left," Sandra Krajicek
Lim, Eddie's cousin and Ed's niece, told me. "But my mother (Ruby
Krajicek, Ed's sister-in-law) always said that when Hazel left that
last time, Uncle Ed waited for some time for her to return. When
she didn't, he took the boys and moved back home with his mother
on South 36th Street. And that was that."

Eddie and Connie didn't have much room to grow in Grandma
Krajicek's little house. In the 1940 Census, the federal government

counted four adults and two children living there: Anna Krajicek, 65; her children Edward, 36, Frank (Darby), 34, and Rose, 32; and her two grandsons, ages 11 and 10. Darby and his brother Red, who lived next door with wife Ruby, operated a bar across the street from the house. (The boys grew up earning spending cash by cleaning up at Darby's Tavern.) Rose had begun her long career as an insurance company secretary in downtown Omaha, and Ed continued his life-long work as a Cudahy's boxmaker. Anna and daughter Rose slept in a tiny front bedroom, the boys shared a second bedroom, and brothers Ed and Frank stayed upstairs, in an unfinished attic space.

Where did Hazel go when she walked out? I imagine that she spent time in Omaha with her sisters. Perhaps she had a boyfriend and bunked with him. But within a matter of months, Hazel put 750 miles between herself and her boys by moving to Detroit, Michigan. Why Detroit? No one seems to know. My guess is that she was following a man. Her brother, John Chandler, also moved to Detroit at about the same time, but his daughter, Marygrace, told me that she believes John followed Hazel, not the other way around. I had assumed that her father was a footloose bachelor when he left Omaha for Michigan. But no. Remarkably, I learned from Marygrace that he, too, had left behind a spouse and children. John's kids were 8, 6, and 4 when he split in late 1936 or early 1937. Runaway parenting was a Chandler family pattern, I'm afraid.

As the siblings settled into their new hometown in May 1937, a sheriff's deputy in Detroit knocked at Hazel's door to serve a court summons calling her back to Omaha, where Ed was suing for divorce, custody of the children and "equitable relief." Oddly, Hazel saved the summons in her little correspondence suitcase. By early summer in 1937, the confused and heart-broken Krajicek boys received their first letters from their mother, postmarked from far, far away.

5707 Poppleton St
Omaha, Nebr.
June 10, 1939

Dear Mother:
How are you? I am sorry
I didn't write sooner. I passed into the seventh grade,
and Connie passed into the
fifth grade. We have a new
cousin and her name is "Sandra
Ann Krajicek." When dad gets
his vacation we might go
fishing to Minesota or go to
Kanas City again to see Jack
and Bob and Monnie. We went
over to grandma's house and
she told me that aunt Pink
sold her house and aunt Fairy
moved

Your son
Edward Krajicek

School Days

July 11, 1937

Dear Mama:

How are you? I passed into the fifth grade. Connie passed into the third grade. Jack passed into the fifth, too. Bob graduated. Jean and Grace passed. [Jack and Bob were Leafy's kids; Jean and Grace were Daisy's.] *Mother, as you asked me in your letter, is Grandma* [Grace Chandler] *home? Yes, she is home. She is all right, too.*

Mama, I don't want nothing for my birthday. Mama, Connie is a bad boy. He won't even go to Mass on Sunday. Connie has the whooping cough. I would send you my picture if I had one to send you. Mama, send me your picture if you can. That will be a birthday present from you to me.

Your loving son,
Edward Krajicek

February 24, 1938

Dear Mama:

    How are you? I go to school every day. I am an altar boy. I serve Mass on Sunday. I joined radio Orphan Annie's Secret Society Club. I have a secret club book and pin. I can read all the secret messages. Alvin Shoehigh, he has them, too. I still play with Bill Gillogly. Little Judy [a Krajicek cousin] *weighs 10 ½ pounds. She is 2 months old. She has black hair and dark eyes. We all love her very much. Bill Slegl* [a Krajicek uncle] *is putting an upstairs in his house. I saw the rooms. They all are very nice.*

Your Loving Son,
Edward Krajicek

February 24, 1938

Dear Mama:

    I have a pair of ice skates. I have a pair of snow runners. I have a friend named Henry Hartnett. He has a Streamline sled. He takes accordion lessons. I carry his accordion home for him and to school for him. I got 65 in reading and spelling.

Love from Conrad to Mama
I love you. Be a good girl. Love me.

June 20, 1938

Dear Mama:

    How are you? I am sorry I didn't write sooner. I would of had a letter mailed already but I lost the letter. I am going to Kury Park today. I am going with Connie and Billy Gillogly. The city fixed Seymour Lake into a swimming pool. They named it Ralston Park Swimming Pool. I went there Sunday. I went with Connie and Dad. It is a very nice place to swim. I got a new swimming suit. I paid $1.95 for it.

Connie got one too. Little Judy has a sore on her head. The doctor come and take a hot iron and burned it. She weighs 17 pounds. I passed into the sixth grade. Connie passed into the fourth.

Your loving son,
Edward Krajicek

November 12, 1938

Dear Ma:

How are you? I am all right. I had a letter all written and Connie did, too, but neither one of us would mail it. We kept putting it off and then we finally lost it. So I had to write another one. We still have our bicycle. I haven't been over to grandmother's since you was there [for a visit]. How do you like it in Detroit? Down here in Omaha the weather is getting pretty cold. Is it very cold up there in Detroit? Connie and I are getting along just fine in school. Did you get a job since you went back to Detroit? I still have the wristwatch that you gave me when you came to Omaha. I know that Connie lost the little wheel at the top of the watch. Well, I haven't any more to say, so I will have to close my letter.

"Love,"
Edward Krajicek

November 12, 1938

Dear Ma:

How are you? For my birthday I got a new pair of gloves. I have a new turnover tank. I could not write to you because I did not know your address. Sonny Hartnett's birthday is on the same day. I have a new American roller game. I got a very pretty birthday cake. It has pumpkin and witches.

Your son,
Conrad Krajicek
Love to you

December 19, 1938

Dear Ma:

How are you? I am not so good. I have an infected left leg, and I can't walk on it. And at the same time I have impetigo [he spelled it "infantigo"] *on my nose, mouth, and on my ear. I can't go to school. In your letter you asked me what I wanted for Christmas. Well, I want a pair of house slippers. On December 1 the doctor had to come and look at my leg. I forgot what his name was. I already got for Christmas a $5 pair of shoe skates and a $13 fur jacket. Connie and I are going to make our Confirmation on December the eighteenth at 4 o'clock in the afternoon at St. Mary's School.*

Your loving son,

Edward Krajicek

P.S. My Confirmation name is Francis. [Catholics choose a second middle name for Confirmation, a sacrament of initiation into the church; Eddie chose his father's middle name.]

December 19, 1938

Dear Mama:

How are you? I got a new overcoat Saturday night. I got a punching bag. I am making my Confirmation Sunday at 4 o'clock. I have a sore nose. And foot. There is going to be a play at Saint Peter and Paul the same day we make our Confirmation.

Love,

Connie

June 10, 1939

Dear Mother:

How are you? I am sorry I didn't write sooner. I passed into the seventh grade, and Connie passed into the fifth grade. We have a new cousin and her name is

Sandra Ann Krajicek. [The first-born child of his Uncle Red and Aunt Ruby Krajicek, who lived next door on South 36th Street.] *When dad gets his vacation we might go fishing to Minnesota or go to Kansas City again to see Jack and Bob and Minnie.* [Leafy Eggleston's boys and the card sharp.] *We went over to grandma's house and she told me that Aunt Pink* [a Chandler cousin] *sold her house and Aunt Daisy moved.*

Your son,

Edward Krajicek

June 13, 1939

Dear Mother:

    How are you? Dad said he was going to take a picture of me and Edward but he never had time, but he said when he has time he will. I passed into the fifth grade. I know how to play a piano. I learned myself how. I can only write a short letter because it's 9:30 and my bedtime is at 9 o'clock.

Your son Conrad

I love you, Mother

October 3, 1939

Dear Ma:

    How are you? We have started back to school, and I am in the seventh grade. I was mascot for a ball team and they were the city champions. Judy is about 1 ½ years old, and she is beginning to talk. Sandra is growing fast, too. My cousin Peppers went up town and someone stole his bike.

Your loving son,

Edward Krajicek

October 13, 1939

Dear Ma:

How are you? Me and my old pal Sonny Hartnett is saving our money and we are going to buy some machinery and put it down his cellar and we can make lots of stuff and maybe we may make you something. Two more weeks and it's my birthday. Sonny used to play with Jack Logan but now he plays with me. Jack got mad because I cut in and begged Sonny to play with me. Now me and him are good friends again. I used to play with them but Jack got mad at me and told me not to come down any more so I didn't.

> Your son Conrad
> I love you.

February 9, 1940

Dear Ma:

How are you? I am sorry that I didn't write sooner. I go ice skating every night after school. When I do get started on a letter I never get it done because I keep doing it over and over, and before you know it I lose it. You asked me what I wanted. Well, I want a pair of "figure skates," but if they cost too much you can send me a pair of mittens. There were two boys sleigh-riding and they were going down a hill and at the bottom of the hill there was a crossing and the bus was coming. One boy rolled off the sled into the path of the bus and the other boy went straight in front of the bus and as he was passing he hit his foot on the wheel of the bus and hurt his ankle. I have the "mumps" and I hope you can read my writing.

> Affectionately,
> Edward Krajicek

August. 23, 1940

Dear Mother:

   How are you? You sent me a wonderful camera. I have took some swell pictures with it. I am sending you some pictures that I took with it. The Boy Scouts went on an overnight hike and we had lots of fun. We are going out to Camp Wilderness [in Fremont, Nebraska, 40 miles from home] on Friday, Saturday, and Sunday, the 30th, 31st, and 1st. I was going to wait to write until after I come home from camp, but I am writing now after camp. School is going to start September 5th or the 9th.

Your loving son,
Edward Lee Krajicek

January 22, 1941

Dear Ma:

   How are you? I got a pair of skis for Christmas, and house slippers, speedometer and mirror for the bike. My aunt gave me a cap. My Aunt Jean gave me a fountain pen. Eddie gave me two books. My Aunt Ruby got a new baby [Paul Krajicek]. It looks just like Red. I got the accordion all right but no book. Will you send me a book? If you get any stamps of any kind that you don't want send them, too. Everybody is just fine. We went over to see Daisy and Grandma about two weeks ago. From there we went down to that café across from Grandma's. We played a new game. It's a gun inside of a tin thing with glass over the top. You shoot the gun and if you hit the target a steely will roll down. Grandma wouldn't let me get a BB gun because when Red was small he had one and got hurt, and Eddie broke Darby's window in the saloon. I just went skating twice this year. Maybe I will go again. We had exams and my lowest grade is 72 so far. The highest is 85. Eddie is in the 8th grade, and I am in the 6th.

With love,
Your son Conrad

Miss. Hazel Krajick
657- Connor Ave.
Detroit, Mich.

Hazle Krajick
987- Selden Ave.
Detroit, Mich.

Hazle Krajick
1790 West Handcock
Detroit, Mich.

Growing Up

I'M SURPRISED THAT SO MANY of her sons' letters found Hazel in Detroit. She was a moving target, with at least a half-dozen different addresses between the summer of 1938 and spring of 1942. I tracked her accommodations based on the letters, and she wasn't living next door to Henry Ford's mansion. Most of her homes were in gritty precincts at the fringes of downtown.

Her first address in Detroit seemed to be at 255 East Vernor Highway, a busy main drag through downtown. She lived along a stretch that was later obliterated for the construction of Interstate 75. By Thanksgiving 1938, Hazel was living at 657 Conner Street, in the heavily industrialized Conner Creek neighborhood. That area featured the same sort of shotgun shacks she grew up around in South Omaha. It had one nice feature: Hazel could have walked six blocks to the Detroit River and gazed across the filthy water to Windsor, Ontario, Canada.

In June 1939, the boys' letters were addressed to Hazel at 987 Selden Street, across from Thomas Jefferson Intermediate School. A year later, she had moved a mile away, to 1790 West Hancock Street.

The address is now a vacant lot, like much of arson-plagued inner-city Detroit. But it stands out on the map of her Detroit domiciles because it is located in Woodbridge, an historic neighborhood of grand Victorian mansions that was still in its prime in the 1940s. I doubt that Hazel was leasing one of the stately old houses, so let's assume she was a lodger renting a room—or working as a live-in maid. In either case, she had moved yet again within six or eight months.

It seems likely that Hazel was living with or near her brother, John, during some of these stops; a few letters to Hazel that I found in the suitcase from her mother and sisters inquire about John. But I can confirm that they were not living together in 1940 when the federal government made its 10-year count of the American population. On April 19 that year, John Chandler was living under lock and key at the Wayne County Jail in Downtown Detroit. He was among nearly 400 men counted in the jail that day. Chandler was 33 years old, and he told the enumerator that he had dropped out of high school after two years (just like Hazel). Those are about the only details on the Census document, which did not specify his charges or sentence. He was either awaiting adjudication of his case or was serving out a sentence of less than one year; he would have been sent to state prison to serve a longer sentence for a serious crime.

Like his sibling sisters, John Chandler had led a life roiled with trouble and tragedy. Born in 1907, the blue-eyed boy had grown into a big, handsome teenager. His life was untracked in the mid-1920s when he was seriously injured in a car accident. A knock to the head caused neurological issues that would dog him forever. After a stretch in the Nebraska state mental hospital in Lincoln, he turned to alcohol to ease his pain, according to his daughter, Marygrace. She told me that his migration to Detroit was an escape from South Omaha, just as it was for Hazel. But his drinking only got worse there, and he lost himself on boozy Michigan Avenue, Detroit's Skid Row. "Sometimes he was good, and sometimes he wasn't," Marygrace said. "It was a sad life." I learned that it did not end well, as we will see.

* * *

I found another surprise in the 1940 Census. Hazel had been receiving letters throughout much of 1940 and '41 at 3023 Putnam Street, another grim corner of the city that was eventually demolished for a highway. Someone, perhaps John, must have been passing her mail along because the Census recorded her as living at another address with her "husband" in Detroit on April 16, 1940, three days before her brother was counted in jail. Public records do not confirm the marriage, so it likely was another Chandler make-believe nuptial. Her supposed spouse was a German immigrant named Bob Beron. He was 39 and Hazel 31. They were living together in an apartment building at 1776 West Warren Avenue in Detroit, and they told the Census-taker that they were married. According to the Census document, Beron worked as a restaurant cook and reported income of $1,560 in 1939 — 30 bucks a week. He apparently was able to fully support Hazel with that meager salary because she told the enumerator that she had no job — and wasn't looking for one. She stuck to that model most of her life.

The relationship with Beron, whatever its legal status, offered some stability to Hazel's life after several years of disruptive movement. She and Bob Beron seemed to be living together at that same apartment for more than five years; Hazel was receiving letters there as late as 1946. Her sisters and mother addressed them to Hazel Beron. Eddie addressed a single letter during those years to the misspelled Hazel Baron. To her boys, she was still Hazel Krajicek.

Oh, about Connie's much-discussed accordion? You may not be surprised that he never learned to play the instrument. It sat on a shelf at his father's house on South 36th Street for more than 50 years. When Grandpa Krajicek died in the 1990s, I inherited the little squeeze box and brought it home to New York, where it has sat on a shelf in my home for the past 25 years—still unplayed except for two brief whirls with accordionists who happened to be visiting. It works just fine. Thanks, Hazel.

Connie's Accordion

January 23, 1941

Dear Mother:

How are you? I was over to Daisy's house but Jean [her daughter] *was at church so we stayed awhile and visited Daisy and then we went over to Grandmother's house. Connie's letter will probably reach you sooner than mine because he wrote his letter Wednesday. I was going to write mine too but I had to go to the Boy Scout meeting.*

Connie and I got a hat, a pair of gloves and a suit from Darby [their Uncle Frank Krajicek]*, but they were different. Connie got a blue suit and a blue hat, and I got a green suit and a pair of brown mittens, and Connie got black finger gloves. My hat was brown with a green band with white dots around it. We got a pair of skis from dad and also a speedometer and a mirror for the bike. I got a Boy Scout suit from Dad. We both got a pair of house slippers from Rose* [their Aunt Rose Krajicek]*. Connie got a blue fountain pen with his name on it, and I got one with my name on it and it was brown.*

All of the Boy Scouts are going to receive Communion at the Cathedral February 9th at the 8 o'clock Mass, and after Mass we are going down to the Henshaw Cafeteria [a popular restaurant in downtown Omaha] *for breakfast. June 16th we are going to Camp Wilderness in Fremont again. It snowed the 22nd and 23rd here. The city has flooded Brown Park for skating. We were only sleigh riding two or three times.*

Yours sincerely,

Edward L. Krajicek

February 14, 1941

Dear Ma:

How are you? It is pretty cold here. It snowed the 12th and there is still some snow on the ground. I would send you my picture but I can't very well take my picture now. But when it gets nicer I will have my picture taken and send it to you. Ruth and I are going to be Godmother and Godfather for Red's baby boy. I think they are going to name him Paul Donald. The eighth-grade boys are going to give the girls in our room a party on Valentine's Day. They gave us a Thanksgiving party so now we are going to give them a party.

Loving,
Edward Krajicek

June 26, 1941

Dear Mother:

How are you? I wrote you a letter but I don't know if you received it because I sent it to your former address.

I graduated. I will start South High next fall. I got a watch and a knife and a chain. I also got a suit and a pair of shoes. Connie passed and he is now in the seventh grade. I had my picture taken but I don't get them until July 3. I will send you one as soon as I get them because I told the woman to mail one of them to you. Dad's vacation starts the 29th of this month, but I don't know if we are going anyplace.

We have an American Legion team and we are the Larkins because Mr. Larkin [owner of a South Omaha funeral home] *is backing us up. We won two games and lost one.*

Yours truly,
Edw. Lee Krajicek

September 2, 1941

Dear Ma:

How are you? I will start South High on September 10, and Connie will start the seventh grade on the 4th of this month. Connie was sick the last few days, but he is all right now. He had to see the doctor Saturday.

Darby went to Minnesota a couple of days ago with John Sewtuck. I was going with him but school will start too soon. Goodbye. I will write again soon.

Happy Birthday,
Eddie

September 30, 1941

Dear Ma:

  How are you? Well, I started high school and I sure do like it. I have taken up a College Preparatory course and the only hard thing I have is Algebra. I have also taken up choric arts, which is about speaking. I took up Elementary Physical Science, which covers all the sciences. We do most of our studying about the stars and planets. We also see a lot of slides. I also have English. I took up music and all we do in there is sing.

  I didn't get lost once, but the only mistake I made was I went to . . .

[Eddie's high school report ended there — unfinished and perhaps hastily mailed. Connie's letter below was in the same envelope]

September 30, 1941

Dear Mother:

  How are you? I joined the Boy Scouts two weeks ago and I like them. The last meeting we played steal the bacon. It was fun. The first meeting I went to we told Robert Eftainer (he is one of my classmates) to turn off the lights. He did it, and Hank and I were wrestling when the lights were turned on. Hank and I were laying on the floor. I had my leg around his head and he had his around mine. Hank's Uncle Frank died, but they were happy. Hartnetts got a dog and named him after ours—anyway, the one we had. I was sick about a month ago and I had to go to the doctor. He gave me some nose drops and one of those things you put on your head. After one night in bed I was all right. I was sick for two days. I thought I had a headache but I found out it was a fever. I am in the Safety Patrol. I and Hank were one of the nine and all the rest of the class were in the Fire Patrol. Today we got our new badges. They are just like the captain's. We did not have the sister [nun] we thought we would have. This one is mean but she is OK sometimes. Hank sits in back of me and Francis Lukowski sits in front of me. Francis is nice and fat but anyhow all three of us talk all day long. But Luke is a nice guy. Luke is a nickname for Francis Lukowski. I would like to have a BB gun with a telescope on the top.

Your loving son,
Conrad

March 4, 1942

Dear Mother:

I am sorry that I didn't write sooner but I couldn't find anything to write about.

I am 9B but I will be a 9C [class designations?] *beginning Monday, March 9. For everyone but me it was hard to sign up. It was no trouble for me that last time. It took me only 20 minutes to sign up and get a locker while it took other kids an hour or so to sign up.*

Mr. Smith is my science teacher and Mrs. Benson is our sponsor.

I played with the South High freshman basketball team and we ended up runner-up for the title. Mr. Moore, a drafting teacher, was our coach.

E. Krajicek

March 4, 1942

Dear Mother:

I am a Boy Scout now. Anyway, I think I am. Hank Hartnett is a patrol leader and his father is the treasurer. Mr. Brown is assistant scout leader and Jim Zack is Scout leader. Hank and I have a squadron of airplanes and we call it the comet squadron. I just learned how to make them and Eddie made one the same time I did and his flew farther than any plane I ever saw and mine didn't. But I made two of them that fly and I sure am proud of them. We have about 20 planes that will take about 2 weeks to make. Every night before I go down to make them I stop at Wisniski's to box. You know who Wisniski is.

They are the ones who came to see you with me last time you were here. I wrote this letter during school time because I hardly have time after school because I am always down at Hank's working on planes. We got about 11 made and have about 11 to make. And after supper I have to do my homework. Dad told me last night that if you would go 50-50 he would get me a new bike because my other one is broke.

If I get one he will have the old one repaired for Eddie. If you are going 50-50 with dad please send about 15 or 20 dollars. But if you can't afford it you don't have to. I am sorry that I didn't write sooner but I did not have anything to say. Frank Acquazzino joined the Navy. He is a kid about 17 years old who lives by us. Everyone is surprised that he joined. Before he joined, we always went riding in his father's car.

Your loving son,

Conrad

XXXXXXXXXXX

Please send the money as soon as you can.

June 26, 1942

Dear Ma:

How are you? We went after a bike but we could not get one. I know everything about a bike and can fix anything on it. I passed into the eighth grade, but I do not think that I am going to St. Mary's School anymore. I quit the Safety Patrol about two weeks before school let out because Sister Ann made me write 2,000 penances for not having my patrol belt washed but I didn't do it and quit. I will send you some pictures of me and Eddie. I am not a Boy Scout anymore, so I have no suit. The only reason I quit is because all they do at meetings is fool around and that's no fun. Well, I guess that's all I have to say. I like the BB gun fine and so does everyone else around our house but I never have any BBs.

With love,

Conrad

June 26, 1942

Dear Ma:

How are you? We are all feeling fine. We had a terrible wind and rainstorm here Friday night. It broke a lot of trees and killed a large number of birds. Everyone in the house was up and they had the lights on, but I didn't hear anything. They said I sat up in bed and said something and then went back to sleep again, but I don't remember doing it.

Morton Park is open but I don't go swimming half as much as I did last year. I went swimming a few weeks ago out to Merritt Beach, and it sure is swell out there.

We have an American Legion baseball team and two of our games have been rained out. It sure has been rainy and wet here this year. When we start back to school I will be in tenth and Connie will be in the eighth grade.

You asked me what I would like to have for my birthday. I would like to have a small portable radio but I suppose it would cost too much money. But outside of that I would like to have some kind of sweater. I will send you some pictures of Connie and me.

> *Yours truly,*
> *Edward*

August 13, 1942

Dear Ma:

How are you? I am feeling fine.

Well, it won't be long now before school starts. I am very anxious to start back to school. I am going back to South and will be a sophomore. I am going to take ROTC this year. I am now 5 feet 5 inches tall and I weigh about 118 pounds.

My Uncle Frank is in the Army. He is now in Camp Carson, Colorado. This is a new camp, and there is still some construction work going on. When it is finished it will house about 50,000 men. It has only about 5,000 men in it now. When he left home he went to Fort Leavenworth, Kansas, and from there he was sent to Camp

Carson. When he was on the train the Army didn't tell him where he was going and he didn't find out until they told him when he got off of the train. He sent me a sweatshirt from Kansas.

I don't go swimming so very much anymore. I can swim 25 yards in 13 and eight-tenths seconds. We are going to have a water carnival August 23 and there will be diving, racing, and comedy acts. There will be prizes given away. It will be sponsored by the Q Street Merchants. I will be in the diving and racing contests.

I am working in the tavern in the mornings, and I will have about $35 saved when school starts. I am going to buy my clothes and things for school. Connie and I are going to buy a bond with the money we have in the bank.

Love,
Eddie

September 9, 1942

Dear Ma:

How are you? Today was a terrible day. It started to rain about 2 o'clock and still is sprinkling, and it is ten after seven. About two weeks ago I had a bike accident and got all scarred up. The fork on my bike broke while I was going around a corner. And about a week later Morton Park had a water carnival. It was really good. Darby wrote home. He is in Camp Carson, Colorado. Tomorrow school starts for me. I am going into the eighth grade. The vacation seemed very short, and I am not going to like school. Do you remember that Boy Scout photograph book you sent Eddie a long time ago? We are starting to fill it with pictures. Darby sent Grandma a marble lighthouse sitting on a mountain. It has little steps on it and a bridge and a little door. That's all.

Your son
With love,
Conrad

October 14, 1942

Dear Ma:

How are you? I am feeling fine. All the schools are bringing in scrap [metal, as part of nationwide World War II initiative]. St. Mary's has more than any school around here. Hank and I brought in about 500 pounds of scrap and still have about 700 pounds to get. I wrote a letter to Darby Tuesday. He is still in Camp Carson, Colorado. He sent us about 20 pictures of himself and one big one for the saloon. Well, my birthday is coming soon, and I will be 13 and Hank will be 15. School is getting to be fun now that it is my last year. Sister Ann isn't so bad. [He apparently had recovered from their dispute over her Safety Patrol "penances."] I had to stay after school and do a couple of arithmetic problems I got wrong. I would have had to stay about an hour but before I was half finished she said we could go if we went to church that morning. I went to church so I got to go home. For my birthday I would like to have a portable radio like Hank has, if it doesn't cost too much. I got to visit Grandma quite often, and I am going Saturday to see her again. Well, I guess I haven't much more to say, so goodbye.

With love, XXXXX
Conrad

November 4, 1942

Dear Mother:

How are you? I hope you are feeling fine. I received the radio in perfect condition. Everyone likes it. It sure is a swell one. I do my homework more often now. I sit and have it in front of me and listen to it. We got a letter from Darby today. He says he is coming home for Christmas.

Soldiers and marines are all over Nebraska. Henry Hartnett lives somewhere near Grandma [Chandler]. He says he likes my radio better

than he does his. I am listening to it now. I just got done with my
homework and so I decided to write you a letter and here it is. It isn't
much of a letter but it will let you know I am well and so is Eddie.
Dad and I fixed the chicken house today. Every morning when I get
up I dress and eat and then I give both the big and little chickens
water because Grandma [Anna Krajicek] is not able to do that. The
doctor said she had to stay in bed on account of her leg. It has been
pretty windy out today but not very cold. Well I guess that is all that
I have to say.

I will write soon.

With love,

Connie

February 1, 1943

[Valentine's Card]

Dear Ma:

We are feeling fine. I hope you are feeling the same. The weather was
nice Sunday and Monday, but Tuesday it was drizzly and
Wednesday it was about zero. The wind up in Colorado is so strong it
almost blew over the camp.

Connie XXX

September 12, 1943

Dear Ma:

Well, I'm in South High now, and I am really glad to get out of
grade school. Here are all my studies: 1st period, study hall; 2nd
period, English; 3rd period, Chorus; 4th period, drafting; 5th period,
lunch; 6th period, study hall; 7th period, study hall; 8th period,
physical science; 9th period, algebra. It's raining cats and dogs out.
It's also windy and cold.

My cousins are over. Godfrey had to close the saloon today because he ran out of beer. He's closed up a couple of times on account of beer. You remember the Wisniski's—you know, Frank, John and Joe, don't you? Well, Joe was drafted and is home on furlough for the first time.

Grace [Daisy's daughter] came home in case you didn't know. Leafy is here, too. Hank lives near Gram so I see her quite often.

Frank Acquazzino, a friend of mine who is in the Navy, has been in the Hawaiian Islands for nearly a year and sevens months and finally got a furlough. Yesterday his mother got a telegram which said he was on his way home. I'm sorry I didn't send you anything for your birthday, but I found out a few days after. Next time I write I'll send you $10. That's all I have to say for a while.

> Your son,
> Conrad

October 4, 1943

Dear Mother:

I suppose you don't think much of me because I haven't written to you for so long, but . . . Well, I won't try to make up any excuses, but I'll promise to try real hard to write you regular.

I'm back in school now and I'm an 11A. I hope I get enough courage to go to Creighton Prep [a more prestigious but rigorous Catholic high school] before this year is over or at the latest next year. I'm in the ROTC again this year and I am a staff sergeant. If I am there next year I will be an officer, so you see that is why it is so hard for me to make up my mind whether to switch schools or not.

Well, Frank Acquazzino came home but he is not on furlough. When he came back to the States he was told to report to Michigan or Minnesota officers training school on October 14, and they called that delayed orders.

Well, that's about all I have to say and will write again soon.

> Your Loving Son,
> Eddie

August 8, 1945

Dear Ma:

I received your letter last week and I think it's about time I answered. Well, I got my horse and now I'm satisfied. It's a nice-looking horse and has got a lot of speed.

Alice moved in with Lorraine right after you left. We met one night and settled our argument, and now we are going steady. I get our car every Sunday afternoon, and Alice and I and a couple of guys and gals from the neighborhood go swimming out at Peony or Merritt's.

Eddie bought a car for $130 ($40 of which was mine) and left for Lake Okoboji over in Iowa about 180 miles from here. He should be home today.

Today's Alice's birthday. She's 16 years old. She wanted a pair of earrings, so I went up to Frank's Jewelry and bought her a pair for $15. Well ma, that's about all I can think of now so with these words I close.

With all my love,
Connie

December 28, 1945

Dear Mom:

Not hearing from you very often makes it very difficult for me to write.

By the way, I saw Grace [Daisy's older daughter] while she was here. She sure looks swell, just as big as ever. I've been going down to Granny's quite often lately. She looks fine and is in the best of health.

I went to work down to Swifts [packinghouse], but it was too darn hard so I quit on the second day. You see mom I'm practically wasting down to a shadow. I only weigh 187 pounds and I'm 6 feet tall. Not bad for a kid, huh? I'm sorry that I never sent you anything for Xmas, but your five bucks came in handy. Thanks! There's really not much that I can write about. Ed said to say hello and that he hopes you're in the best of health.

I sure wish that you would come home, mom. It would seem just grand to see you once again.

It's pretty late, mom, as I just got home from the show. Oh! I forgot to tell you that I'm going steady with the most wonderful girl in the world. I bought her a 17-jewel Bulova with a few diamonds in it. You see, that's what got me in the hole for Christmas. Well, I guess that's about all. Write soon.

Love,
Connie

P.S. I miss you, mom . . .

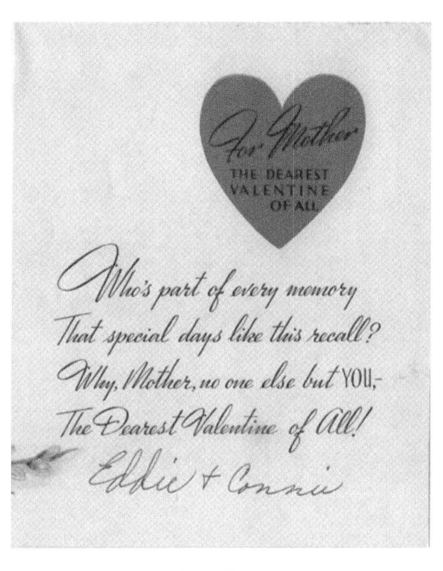

For Mother
THE DEAREST
VALENTINE
OF ALL

Who's part of every memory
That special days like this recall?
Why, Mother, no one else but YOU,-
The Dearest Valentine of All!

Eddie & Connie

Valentine's Day, 1943

Connie and Eddie's Confirmation, 1938

'Awful Lonesome'

CONNIE WAS 16 YEARS OLD when he sent the letter to his mother at Christmastime in 1945, the last from him that I found in Hazel's little suitcase. It would soon become pertinent that he told Hazel that he'd visited Grandma Grace Chandler and found her "in the best of health." If that was true, Grace was hiding a secret from her grandson. Hazel's suitcase trove included two envelopes mailed to her and Bob Beron in Detroit from her mother in South Omaha. One envelope, postmarked December 1, 1945, was empty, unfortunately. The second contained a very revealing letter. It was dated December 21, 1945, exactly a week before Connie's note. In the letter, Grace revealed to Hazel (using her nickname, "Hootie") that she was broke and miserable.

My Dear Hootie & Bob: I just got your card and 10 dollars and thanks but Hootie I am always afraid you can't spare it but anyway I got it. Hootie, I can't send you anything this time & I think it is foolish to send these cards, but maybe after they let things come back [World War II had just ended] *I'll send you something nice . . . Connie comes over all the time and tells me everything. They are fine now. Do you ever see John? I got a card from him & I am going to rite to him rite away. How is Bob? I hope fine. Daisy is running the restaurant in Vail. It has been awful cold here – 20 below but warmer today . . . Now Hootie I can't buy a stocking or socks or anything but after the 1st of the year I can so I'll send you something nice . . . It is awful lonesome here around the holidays. Anyway, I sure wish you and Big Bob could live here with me. Tell Bob hello and maybe you and him can come home sometime. I sure hope so. Now Honey I'll send something later so don't be mad. You rite to me anyway. Love Ma & thanks again. Merry Xmas & New Year. By-by Honey & thanks. Love Ma to Bob & Hootie*

The handwriting got larger, looser, and more crooked as the letter went on, suggesting that Grace Chandler was drinking. By that date, she had left her South 23rd Street house and was living in beggar's quarters at 5413 South 28th Avenue, in the meatpacking district housing projects. She apparently had a paid boarder named August Teckmeyer. On New Year's Eve 1945, days after she complained of loneliness in the letter to Hazel, someone smelled gas coming from her apartment. Inside, rescuers found Teckmeyer, 46, dead of carbon monoxide poisoning and Grace clinging to life. She was swept off to a hospital, where she died two days later, at age 65. A brief story in the *Omaha World-Herald* said the "illuminating gas" had emanated from a kitchen stove jet that was open but unlit—a common method of both accidental and on-purpose deaths in that era. Marygrace Chandler Hansen shared her grandmother's death certificate with me. Dr. Walsh, Grace's attending physician at Omaha's old Doctor's Hospital, wrote the following on the document as the "immediate cause of death": "Illuminating gas poisoning. Accidental gas poisoning." The fact that the doctor wrote the phrase twice to specify "accidental" seems like a pointed decision to clear up any ambiguity. But as is often the case, the Chandlers had another version of Grace's death that has been passed down.

This lore is centered on Bert Brown, Grace's son, who was a police detective sergeant in Omaha at the time. According to the story, Bert whispered the inside cop gossip that Grace's apartment had been staged for a gas suicide, with newspapers stuffed into gaps around the windows to impede the flow of fresh air. Which story should be believed? On the one hand, Grace's final letter to "Hootie" made clear that she was depressed. But the window stuffing might have been to keep a drafty apartment warm as winter's cold set in. I trust the doctor's assessment of accidental poisoning. But either way, I'm certain Hazel must have felt grief and guilt.

I found one other curiosity in Grace's passing. Both the brief newspaper story and the death certificate identified the victim as "Mrs. Grace Chandler Gregerson" — a mysterious surname. Bob Haukap told me this was likely another example of a Chandler fairy-tale marriage. In her last years, Grace sometimes lived with a man named Lou Gregerson, Haukap said. She probably used his name to bring legitimacy to the relationship, in the custom back then. But it seems perfectly appropriate that Grandma Grace would sail off into eternity with a pseudonym on her official departure document.

Grace Chandler and Hazel with a nephew, South Omaha, 1945

As the drama of her death was playing out, Grace's grandson Eddie was struggling with an existential crisis. He was a good student and an ambitious teenager. He excelled at his public high school, but he somehow had become convinced that his path to a successful life would be straighter if he transferred to Creighton Prep, a locally renowned but rigorous private Jesuit high school located halfway across town, nearly 10 miles from home. Eddie wrestled mightily with the idea of transferring after his sophomore and junior years at South High. Tellingly, in his letter to Hazel in 1943, he admitted that he was trying to "get enough courage" to switch to Prep. The school transfer dilemma was directly linked to another of his ambitions — to become a pharmacist. He mentions this plan repeatedly in letters to his mother during his stint in the Navy.

I've often wondered where he got that idea since no one in the family worked in that profession. Our people were meatpackers and saloonkeepers, not college stock. But I think my snooping may have solved another minor mystery. Eddie attended school and services at St. Mary's Catholic Church, at 36th and Q Streets. The membership there during the 1940s included a couple named Julius and Ruth Deslee and their two children. Julius, the son of Belgian immigrants, was a college-trained druggist who owned and operated Deslee Pharmacy, at 3901 Q Street, eight blocks from Eddie's home.

I discovered that Julius Deslee had attended pharmacy school at Creighton University in the late 1920s. I believe he became a mentor to teenage Eddie, suggesting that he follow in his footsteps via Creighton. His Navy letters suggest that he and Deslee had discussed the possibility that Eddie would one day buy his pharmacy. He spells this out in a letter to his mother in October 1947, with just two months remaining in his military service. He wrote, *"I'm still going back to Creighton and study pharmacy if Mr. Deslee still wants to sell me his drug store when I get out of school so he can retire."*

Well, he never made it to Creighton Prep, but Eddie Krajicek did graduate from South High and enroll at Creighton University, with pharmacy as his planned course of study. Alas, he lasted only one semester before washing out. As he wrote to Hazel during his military service, *"When I started Creighton I was not interested in school of any kind, but now I can hardly wait to get back."* The Navy was his backup plan.

Besides a divorce summons, Hazel's little suitcase contained just one other communication from her ex-husband. It was a curt letter written in May 1946, a few months after their son enlisted. Hazel apparently had griped that Eddie didn't visit her during his eight weeks of basic training at the Great Lakes naval base near Chicago, 300 miles from Detroit. The front page of Ed's letter was a gruff dismissal of her complaint: "It's your own fault." On the back, his tone softened as he wrote, "The Navy will do Eddie some good. I can tell by the way he writes, and how he was when he was home on his leave."

May 19, 1946
San Diego, California

Dear Mother:

I am very sorry I didn't write sooner. I have sent two letters to you, but they came back. I hope you get this one.

I am now in the Hospital Corps School in San Diego. I have been here for three weeks and I have 5 more to go. I like the school very much. I am going to try and get into [the military's] pharmacy school when I get through here. I hope I can because I plan to go back to college and study pharmacy when I get out of the Navy.

I haven't seen very much of that California sunshine as yet. It is cloudy here most of the time. Our school is in Balboa Park, and it is a very beautiful place. It is only a 5-minute ride to San Diego but I seldom go there. There is nothing to do but go to a show. I hope to go to Hollywood in a few weeks.

Well I have been in the Navy for four months and I have only 20 more to go. It seems like a long time to me. I doubt if I'll ever leave the States, though. I'll be put in a hospital somewhere most likely. I hate to think of spending two years like that. I am going to try and get sea duty in a few months. I would kind of like to see Tokyo before I get out of the Navy. I hope you will excuse the writing because it is worse than usual today. I am a very poor penman anyway.

I feel very guilty when I think of how very seldom I write to you, but I promise I shall write more often in the future.

Well, mom, I know this is not a very good letter, but I can't think of anything to say. I'll write again when I hear from you and I'll try to make it a better letter.

Your son,

Eddie

June 4, 1946
San Diego

Dear Mom:

I received your letter today and I am answering it right away so I don't get behind in writing to you.

I have only 2 ½ weeks left of school and then I'll most likely go to Georgia. I would like to get stationed somewhere in the Middle West but that is too much to hope for. But anyway you don't have to worry about me going overseas. I'll most likely be in schools and hospitals for my two years in the Navy. In a way I would kind of like to go overseas but I doubt I will ever get the chance to.

Well, for the last week or so I have been seeing a lot of the California sunshine, but I had to wait for about four weeks before it came out. This Sunday I am going to Mission Beach and have a nice swim in the ocean. I was out there a couple of weeks ago and I had a lot of fun. I rode on the roller coaster most of the day.

Helen [Strack, his high school sweetheart] also graduated from school. I sent her a nice green wristwatch. Jim didn't graduate, did he?

Now, mom, I am very sorry if I hurt your feelings in my letter. I can assure you, mom dear, I shall never do it again. No one on Q Street or anywhere else could say anything that could make me stop loving you.

Dad always did tell Connie and I to write you, but I guess we were too young to understand. But now I think I know how you feel and I shall write you often, mom. If I ever get anywhere near Detroit again I'll come and see you right away. I am going to take some pictures in a month or so and when I do I'll send them right away to you. As you can see I had to change ink and this is a rather messy letter. I got two letters from Helen today, so I have a lot of writing to do tonight. She writes me every day.

Well, ma, it's time for chow now and my stomach is growling, so I had better get going. I'll write again in a few days.

Your Loving Son,
Eddie

August 1, 1946
Memphis, Tennessee

Dear Mom:

It has been an awfully long time since I have heard from or written you. The last time I got a letter from you was on my birthday. I am quite sure that I answered it and thanked you for the money, but now that I haven't heard from you for so long I am beginning to doubt whether or not I answered your letter. If I didn't I am very, very sorry, mom, and once again I thank you for the $10 you sent me. Helen sent me a real nice toilet bag and a carton of cigarettes. She also sent me some birthday cards.

It is really hot down here in Memphis. But when we have a rain it cools off considerably. We had a light shower today and it is nice and cool now. I went horseback riding for three hours Sunday and I almost ran the horse to death, but the way I felt for a couple of days I am beginning to wonder who got the best end of the deal—me or the horse?

Memphis is a typical sailor town. Wherever you go everyone is trying to take the servicemen's money. I stay on the base most of the time unless I have something to do. As of yesterday I have been in the Navy for six months. I am still editor of the hospital paper and it is a very good job. I have liberty every night and every weekend, and the other guys have every other night and weekend. I hope you can read this; for some reason or another I am writing very small.

There is a show on the base tonight and I am going over to see it in a few minutes. Well, mom, this about all for now so I will close for this time. Mom, if I didn't answer your last letter I am very sorry, and you can be sure it won't happen again.

Love,

Your Son

Eddie

August 22, 1946
Houston, Texas

Dear Mom:

I received your letter yesterday, and I also received a letter today that I wrote you. I put on the wrong address so it was sent back. I am sending it also. It was very stupid of me but it will never happen again.

I am now in Houston, Texas. I was transferred here about two weeks ago. It was hot in Memphis but it is even more so here. I am at a new hospital and it is not all built as yet. We have been cleaning it up since I came here. It is to be commissioned sometime in the first part of next month. It is really a beautiful place. It cost $11 million to build it.

[He was at the U.S. Navy Hospital, which opened two weeks later. Touted as the most modern medical facility in the South, it featured 39 buildings sprawled over 118 acres. Today, it functions as the Houston VA Hospital.]

I do not know as yet where I will work and I don't particularly care. I think at first I will work on the N.P. Ward. That's the ward where they send the patients who are crazy. It is pretty good duty though. I hope to get put in the pharmacy soon but I don't know for sure.

So Jack [Eggleston, his cousin] is back and is getting discharged. That's fine. I sure hope he writes me 'cause I would like to hear from him. Yes, I still write to Helen and I guess I am pretty nuts about her. I hope Connie doesn't join when he is 17 'cause I doubt if he'll like the life of a serviceman. If he does intend to join I am going to try and talk him out of it 'cause it is a heck of a lot better to be home than to be in this Navy.

I sure hope I can get stationed at Great Lakes sometime while I am in 'cause I could come and see you on a weekend, but I doubt if I'll ever be able to get there. If I am not stationed closer to home or at a better place by the first of the year I am going to try and get sea duty. Anything is better than Texas. Ha ha. These Texans are really the most conceited people in all of the world. Well, mom, I have to write Dad now and also Helen and a couple of buddies, so I'll close for now. I'll write again in a few days and I'll also have Connie drop you a few lines. He has a good time with that old car of mine, but he just won't go to work. Ha ha.

Love,

Your Son

Eddie

P.S. I forgot to tell you, mom, that I had some pictures taken in Memphis and I am going to send you a painted one as soon as I get them. They are ready now. One of my buddies is going to send me them. I should have them by Monday so you should get it soon.

Love,

Eddie

Second P.S. I'll write Connie tonight and have him write you. This is a pretty messed up couple of letters, aren't they? Ha ha. But I'll do better next time.

Love,

Eddie

September 5, 1946
Houston, Texas

Dear Mom:

Received your letter today and was glad to know you like it [his "painted" Navy photo?].

Yesterday the hospital was commissioned and we had a couple of admirals here. They gave speeches and the program was rather nice. We have been working day and night for the last six or seven days getting everything ready, but now we just lay *around and take it easy. It is starting to get a little cool here now, but it is about time 'cause I have almost burnt up in the last month down here. I have been in for seven months now and I still have 17 more to go. It doesn't seem like too long and I know I won't mind it too much. One good thing is when I get out I'll have three years of college coming to me under the GI Bill* [signed into law by President Roosevelt in 1944].

I have had an awful cold for the past few days but now it is starting to clear up.

Houston is a beautiful city. Everywhere you look is a park or school. About 10 blocks away is Rice University, and it is one of the most beautiful in the country. They have some football games here, so I hope to see them play a few times this fall. I sent Dad and Helen a picture like yours. I didn't hear from Dad as yet but I know he likes it. He was very anxious to get one I know.

Say, I guess I am a real Texan now that I know my Grandpop [William Chandler] *was born here. These people down here still don't know who won the Civil War. Ha ha. As far as school is concerned I am still stuck on pharmacy and when I get out I am going to work hard to get my degree. When I started Creighton I was not interested in school of any kind but now I can hardly wait to get back.*

Well, mom, I hope you are feeling well and everything is OK, I'll close for now and write again soon.

Love,
Eddie

September 23, 1946
Norfolk, Virginia

Dear Mom:

Well, now I am in Norfolk, Virginia. I sure have been on the move since I have been in the Navy. I'll only be here for a few days though because I am getting my ship Thursday and shipping out Saturday, September 28th. I am really happy about it 'cause it is what I wanted ever since I have been in the Navy. I am going to duty in the South Pacific. We'll go down through the Panama Canal from here and

74

maybe up to Frisco before we go to the Pacific. I hope so 'cause I would really like to see Frisco. I'll be on the USS Lejeune (La-*Joon*), a transport, so I hope to make a few trips to Japan before long. As you know I was in Houston, Texas, for a few months and it is really a beautiful city.

Don't answer this letter because if you send it to me here I doubt if I would ever get it. My address will be changed to Frisco before long and I'll send it to you as soon as I know for sure what it is. I have been on the East Coast for one day now and all I have seen is . . . rain. Well, mom, I am pretty tired now so I think I had better hit the sack before I drop over. We were on the go all day, too. We went over to catch our ship when we got here but our ship left before we got there so that is why we have to wait 'til Thursday to get our ship. It went out for a shakedown cruise for a couple of days.

Well, mom, this is all for now. I'll write in a few days and let you know my address when I get it.

Love,
Your Son
Eddie

September 27, 1946
Aboard the USS Lejeune

Dear Mom:

I am now aboard ship. I'm on the USS Lejeune. We came aboard yesterday noon. This was a German ship but we have converted it into a ship to carry the wives and children of servicemen overseas. It is a pretty good ship but I'll not stay on it permanently. I get off at Frisco and get another ship to the South Pacific. We shove off at 1 o'clock tomorrow afternoon for Panama City. All of the corpsmen are classified as passengers but we still do most of the work around here. Me and a few of my buddies work in the galley washing dishes, and they keep us kind of busy. Ha ha.

Our living compartments are really small. You hardly have room to turn around. Our bunks are four high and I sleep in the top one. In three more days now I will have been in the Navy for eight months. I have 16 left and from the looks of things I am going to spend them on some island. I don't know for sure yet but if I'm lucky I might get to stay on some ship.

The chow so far has been good and since I work in the galley I'll get all I want to eat. We are supposed to hit Frisco or Treasure Island in about 18 days, or else the 13th of October.

My new address will be:

Edward Krajicek, HA 2/C

317-69-74

U.S.S. Lejeune

C/O Fleet Post Office

San Francisco, Calif.

I am feeling fine except for a cold. I guess this is about all for now. I'll write again soon.

Love,

Your Son

Eddie

November 14, 1946
Aboard the USS President Hayes

Dear Mom:

I am now onboard ship. I'm on the President Hayes. We sail in the morning at 10 for Pearl Harbor and we reach it the 21st. I'm still going for further transfers, so that means I'll be there for a couple of days or else a couple of weeks. You never can tell.

I am working in the galley again. I guess they just can't get along without me 'cause both times I've come on ship they put me in there.

I got a bunch of letters from my girl today. I came aboard ship yesterday so I had one of my buddies check my mail at the T.I. for me today before he came aboard and he got some for me. I guess from the way Helen writes she is more lonesome than I am.

Our living quarters here are a little better than they were the last time, but it is sure hot down here. I can just imagine what it will be like when we get somewhere where it's hot.

Well, mom, I guess this is about all for now. I am feeling fine except for this greasy slop they feed us and call chow. Boy, if we have another meal like we had tonight I'll croak. So far that is all I have to crab about, but I'll find a lot more to holler about before long. Ha ha.

Goodbye for now, mom. I hope you are well, and I'll write again soon.

I hope you can read this cause I'm all cramped up in my bunk trying to write.

Love,

Your son

Eddie

My new address is on the envelope.

Envelope 1:
Edward Krajick P... 317-68-74
U. S. N. H. C. B. Co. 45-1
San Diego 34, Calif.

SAN DIEGO
MAY 20
12:00 PM
1946
CALIF.

Air Mail

AIR MAIL 8
UNITED STATES OF AMERICA

Mrs. Hazel Baron
1776 West Warren
Detroit, Michigan

Envelope 2:
...rajick H a 2 317-68-74
...N.H. (Staff) Navy #10
...Aiea Heights (T.H.)
C/o F.P.O. San Francisco, Calif.

U.S. NAVY
NOV 25
11:30AM
1946

VIA AIR MAIL
CORREO AEREO

AIR MAIL 5
UNITED STATES OF AMERICA

Mrs. Hazel Krajick
1776 - W. Warren
Detroit 8, Mich.

PAR
AVION

Envelope 3:
E. Krajick Phos 3
U.S. N. H. #10 T.H.
C/o F.P.O. S.F.

NAVHOSP BR
NOV 12
1947
HONOLULU, T.H.

VIA AIR MAIL →

AIR MAIL 5

Mrs. Hazel Dick
R.R. #3
Gladwin, Mich.

Pearl Harbor Homesick Blues

EDDIE KRAJICEK'S "COUPLE OF DAYS" in Hawaii would turn into a solid year. He had hoped to spend time at sea and visit the world while in the Navy—Japan, the South Pacific, and more. But he spent only a few weeks at sea before getting stuck at a deathly quiet hospital on a hilltop above Pearl Harbor, on the south shore of Oahu. That would become the last stop in his 22 months of military duty. He seemed to hate every minute there. His salvation was sports with other sailors—pickup football, an organized baseball team, bowling, and swimming, one of his other recreational favorites.

He was a victim of his own poor timing. The massive Japanese sneak attack on the Pearl Harbor naval base in December 1941 had prompted the United States to belatedly enter World War II. Just nine months before Pearl Harbor, Congress had authorized construction of a new naval hospital in Aiea, a sugar plantation town that looked down on the harbor from 300 feet above. The facility was rushed into service in 1942, and over the ensuing three years it would treat more than 100,000 Marines and sailors wounded in the

Pacific theater, including nearly 5,700 in a single month, March 1945, while fighting raged at Okinawa and Iwo Jima, Japan. Those would have been exciting but stressful days for the young aspiring pharmacist.

But the war had ended five months before Eddie signed up, and the halls of his sleepy hospital saw more slow-rolling mop buckets than hurtling gurneys. He was just a hike down the hill from vibrant Honolulu, but he rarely went there—even spending New Year's Eve alone in his quarters. He was annoyed that everyone he met in military towns seemed to be trying to get in his wallet. And he suffered through two months of pain after a military dentist "chiseled out" his wisdom teeth. Even Honolulu's famously fine weather—year-round highs in the 80s and lows in the 60s—grated on him. "If it even went one day without raining, I'm sure a holiday would be declared," he wrote in March 1947.

He makes clear in his final letters from Hawaii that he was in a hurry to restart his life—to reunite with "my girl," Helen, and to get back on track with his occupational dream. My stepmother, Beverly, told me that my father said he was allowed to function as a proxy doctor at the base hospital, making decisions about which medications would best treat a fellow sailor's symptoms. Working in the pharmacy was one of the few things he enjoyed about his time in Hawaii. "If I wasn't working there, I would sure try to get off this rock," he wrote.

November 24, 1946
Pearl Harbor, Hawaii

Hello, Mom:
I read your letter Thursday when I was across the way at the Receiving Station, but I waited 'til now to answer because I wanted to know where I was going before I answered it. My traveling days are over for awhile now because I am

stationed here at *Aiea Heights Hospital* in *Pearl Harbor*. *This hospital is a beautiful place way up here in the hills. I have a good view of most of the island from here. It is hot here but up on this hill is cooler than most places on the island. We have all types of recreation here. I was swimming yesterday. We really have a nice pool. I got sunburned but I'll go today and turn tan.*

I started this letter this morning but the guys started a football game, and I couldn't resist it so I went out and played. Later we went swimming and had a lot of fun.

The chow here at this hospital is pretty good. It is a lot better than I have been getting for the last couple of months. We have five washing machines in back of our barracks, so I washed a lot of my dirty clothes.

This weekend has been a nice one for I laid around in the sun and played around all weekend. But tomorrow we will get assigned to our jobs. I hope I don't get ward duty but I'm afraid I will.

I wish I would have known about that radio 'cause I would much rather have had a portable. If I can sell the one I have now I would like to have it, but don't send it unless I ask for it 'cause I won't sell my radio unless I can get what I paid for it.

This isn't a very long letter, mom, but this is about all I can think of now. I'll write again in a few days when I'm more settled. Goodbye for now.

Love,
Your Son
Eddie

December 30, 1946
Pearl Harbor

Hello Mom:

I received your card and the money last week. The card was very nice and thank you for the money, mom. I am off duty tonight but I have to work 'til 9 for the rest of the week 'cause I got four days off for Xmas. I didn't even go on liberty. I laid around the barracks and monkeyed around. Tomorrow is New Year's Eve, but I doubt if I'll even stay up to see the new year in.

I haven't got the radio as yet but it should be here soon. I haven't had any mail since I got your card so it wasn't too much of an Xmas for me. The weather has turned for the better lately and I hope it stays this way. I had planned to swim day and night on my four days off but they closed the pool because of some kind of disease.

I still work on the same ward and now we have two new nurses. A guy on my ward is a pro baseball player, and him and I play catch most every afternoon. It seems good to play ball again. I miss the game now that I can't play it.

Well, mom, I'd like to write a longer letter but I've seemed to run out of things to say. I have to shower, shave, and get ready for tomorrow so I had better close now and get on the ball. I'll write and let you know when the radio gets to me.

Oh, yes, my Uncle Jim [Krajicek] sent me a postal note in an Xmas card, but I can't cash it for it is only good in the States.

Goodnight for now, mom. I'll write again soon.

Love,

Your Son

Eddie

February 23, 1947
Pearl Harbor

Dear Mom:

I received your letter today and I was happy to receive it. I am really sorry it has been so long since I have written. I know it has made you feel bad and I'm sorry mom.

We have been practicing baseball here the last few weeks, and it is the only exercise I've gotten in some time now. I did weigh 170 pounds a while back but I'm down a few pounds now. I had my four wisdom teeth pulled out over a period of a week awhile back and they sure gave me a lot of trouble. It would have been OK but the dentist had to chisel the bottom ones out. He must have slipped on the lower left side 'cause it is still stitched up. I went there 'cause I had one bad tooth to be filled and he pulled 4 of them. I'll never let them get me again, though.

I am working in the pharmacy now and have been for the last month or so, and I sure like to work up there. I hope to learn enough to help me through school when I get out.

Time is slipping by now. I've been in 13 months and with the leave I have coming I'll be out in about 9 months. I'll be glad when I get out of school so I can settle down, I guess.

Oh, I forgot to tell you I have the radio and it is still great. It is really nice and it plays well. I got it about the 12th of January so it must have taken quite some time to get here. I take it to the beach with me all the time. I still haven't seen much of this island but one of these weekends I'll take a trip around the island. It's only 80 miles around.

I received a letter from Connie a few weeks ago and almost fell over. Dad must have stood over him with a shotgun. When I write him I'll tell him to be sure to write to you, mom, or I'll have to work him over when I come back—that is if I still can. From what I hear he is getting bigger all the time. He was always bigger than me the last couple of years. He was helping my Uncle Frank in the saloon a while back and some soldier started some trouble and Connie beat him up, but the only trouble is he got thrown in the jug. Ha ha. He's a pretty tough one, I guess. It must be the Irish in him, huh? Ha ha. He still has the car I gave him when I left and he takes good care of it, although it was never any too good. Send me Daisy's address and when I hit the West Coast I'll go down to L.A. and look her up. I always have wanted to go there. I'm going to the East Coast some day, also. I've been there, but it was Norfolk, Virginia, and I want to go to New York.

[Daisy lived briefly in suburban Riverside, California, east of Los Angeles, with Bert Brown, her half-brother, and his wife, Nellie. Brown, the police detective, was involved in a controversial service-related disability claim in Omaha that was settled in his favor in 1949. By then, he had been living in Riverside for a year, based on a letter I found in Hazel's suitcase . . . The Navy didn't help Eddie get to New York, but he came to visit me there several times decades later. He was awed by the city. Driving over the George Washington

Bridge into upper Manhattan, he shook his head and said with honest wonder, "Who liiiiives in all these buildings!?" He wasn't intimated by New York. In another manifestation of his remarkable empathy, he wanted to get to know everyone who lived there—except the gay hooker who tried to pick him up early one morning near Lincoln Center.]

I am sorry to hear you are sick, mom, but I hope you are well now. Helen was pretty sick a month or so ago. There was something wrong with her throat. She is going to be 19 soon and says she is becoming an old bag. I believe her, too. Ha ha.

Well, mom, this is all for now, and I'll not go so long without writing to you.

Love,

Your Son

Eddie

March 31, 1947

Pearl Harbor

Dear Mom:

I just received your letter a little while ago and was happy to hear from you. I'm writing this early 'cause I have to bowl tonight. We have a league here on the base and when we bowl we have a lot of fun. I should be practicing ball now, but I'm taking a day off to write letters.

The weather here is not much better than that you have had. If it even went one day without raining, I'm sure a holiday would be declared.

We went over to the other side of the island to play ball yesterday, but we were rained out. But the other side is really beautiful. It is all mountains and oceans there.

I only have about seven months to go over here and then I go back to Frisco for leave and discharge. I should be home in eight months at the longest.

I've met a few guys from home here and we really have some real bull sessions when we get started. My teeth are OK now but I think I have to have a couple filled. He really gave me a bad time when he chiseled out my wisdom teeth.

I still work in the pharmacy and I like it a lot. If I wasn't working there I would sure try to get off this rock. I've been in Honolulu twice since I've been here.

I usually go out to the beach somewhere. A lot of the boys are afraid that we are going to war with Russia but I don't know what I think. I just know that the U.S. is taking a lot of baloney from Russia. But I can't talk about it though 'cause I get too wound up over the way things are going. Well, mom, I'm going to chow now, so I'll close for this time.

Love,
Your Son
Eddie

April 21, 1947
Pearl Harbor

Dear Mom:

I'm sorry I haven't written for so long but I keep on the move day and night here for the last few weeks.

We still have our bowling team and we are doing better each week. We sure beat the nurses the other day, and we have been kidding the pants off of them.

Our ball team hasn't been doing so hot, though. We have only won about 3 games and we have lost about 10 or so. I catch most of the time but I also play shortstop and second base. I caught two games over the weekend and I'm really stiff now.

It is getting hotter here as each week passes but I like it 'cause it has been cold here all of the time since I have come. I'm still working in the pharmacy and am beginning to learn quite a lot. I study all of the nights I'm off. There sure is a lot to learn, though. I suppose you haven't heard from Connie as yet. I'll write him soon and give him the word. He is even more lazy than I am.

Well, mom, I've only got about 6 ½ months to go over here and then I'll be back in the States, and then I should be out for good about the first of December. I'll be up to see you when I get back, mom, and Connie will come with me. Well, mom, this is all for now. I'll write again soon.

Love,
Your Son
Eddie

July 29, 1947
Pearl Harbor

Dear Mom:

I received your card and letter today and was very happy to hear from you. Did you get the flowers I sent you for Mother's Day, mom?

Mom, you know I could never be mad at you for marrying again. Mom, as long as you are happy I am glad. You deserve all of the happiness in the world, mom, and I'll come to visit you when I get out—which is only about 5 months from now. Connie did not graduate from school so he is going to summer school. I guess he is kind of footloose yet. I'll get him on the ball though when I get home.

The weather here has been bad lately. It rains most of the time. I took a test for PHM 3/C [pharmacist third class] *last week and I made it, so as of 2 July I'm a rated man. Ha ha. Think I should ship over* [re-enlist]*? That would be the day.*

Well, mom, I guess this is about all for now. Nothing new has happened but a lot of my buddies have gone back to the States for discharge. Goodbye for now, mom. I am fine and hope you are the same. I'll write again soon.

Love,
Your Son
Eddie

October 10, 1947
Pearl Harbor

Dear Mom:

I received your letter today and I'm very sorry I haven't written for so long. I'm still in the same place and things are pretty much the same as always, and I hardly ever write to anyone. All I do is count the days I have to go, with 49 to discharge. I don't think of anything else. I'll be happy to get out of this outfit.

With these meatless days chow is worse than ever but I can stand anything for the short time I have to go. I'm still going back to Creighton and study pharmacy if

Mr. Deslee still wants to sell me his drug store when I get out of school so he can retire. If not, hard telling what I'll do.

I'm still working in the pharmacy here and I have learned a lot in the last 10 months here. I think I can make a fine career as a druggist if I get the chance. Oh, yes. They rated me a couple of months ago. I guess they are trying to tempt me to ship over. What a joke.

Well, mom, how's things with you? I hope you are well. I am fine and getting fat. Jean sure is starting a big family, isn't she? Where is she living now? Is Jack living in KC? Is Hughie in Omaha? [All are Chandler cousins.] *I suppose he is as big as ever, huh? I'd love to see all of them when I get out.*

Well, mom, I guess this is it for now so I'll close for this time. I'll write again soon, mom.

> *Love,*
> *Your Son*
> *Eddie*

November 11, 1947
Pearl Harbor

Dear Mom:

I received your letter a few days ago and was very glad to hear from you again. I suppose it is cold back there by now. It was very hot here until about a week ago, and then it started raining and hasn't quit for long since.

I leave here Friday morning for the Receiving Station to get a ship back to the States. If all goes well I should be out by the end of the month. But there are so many guys getting discharged these days it is hard to say when I'll get out for sure. It is now 4 a.m. and I'm on watch. I don't mind this one though for it is my last one in the Navy. I'm very anxious to get home now, and I hate to think of all the red tape and traveling I have to do in the next 3 weeks.

I haven't heard from dad for a couple of months, but I guess it is because I haven't written. I take it everyone is all right, though.

David J. Krajicek

How are things on the farm with you, mom? I could sure go for some of those chickens on our meatless Tuesdays. These cooks really turn out some weird-looking messes on those days. Today is a holiday, though, so we might have something decent today. I'll only work an hour or so today and then go swimming if it doesn't rain all day again.

Well, mom, I'm fine and hope you are also. Don't write anymore 'til I write again, which I will do when I get home.

Love,

Your Son

Eddie

Pharmacist's Mate Eddie Krajicek, December 1946, Pearl Harbor, Hawaii

Ed Krajicek, Helen Strack, Eddie Krajicek, South Omaha, 1949

Bye for Now

EDDIE KRAJICEK'S MILITARY TORTURE FINALLY ENDED, and he returned home to Omaha—and his sweetheart Helen—just before
Christmas in 1947. He must have smiled when he learned that the
Navy closed his Hawaii hospital about 18 months after he shipped
out. He came home determined to use the GI Bill to pay for his college education, but real life had other plans.

My father proposed to Helen sometime the following year, and
their wedding would be no Council Bluffs quickie. It was a full-
blown South Omaha Catholic event, held at St. Anthony's, the
church Helen attended, a block up the hill from her home at 3014 S
Street. It was planned for more than a year—and announced with a
proper story in the *World-Herald*. To the ever-dutiful Eddie, spending three or more years in college at that point must have seemed
unjustifiable. He was going to be married; there would be bills to
pay. So both he and Helen went to work—at Cudahy's packinghouse, like his father. My dad would go on to live a successful,
prosperous life, but I sense he always regretted that his dream of a
career as a pharmacist drifted out of his grasp.

Eddie and Helen were married on June 18, 1949. The newspaper announcement was largely a marvelously baroque description of the wedding dress. "Such was the fashion then," as my sister Julie Krajicek put it. It read, "The bride's gown of white lace over satin was fashioned with a fitted bodice, an off-shoulder yoke outlined by a ruffle, and a three-yard train. Her fingertip veil of illusion fell from a lace bonnet. She carried white carnations and lilies of the valley." Her maid of honor, little sister Eileen Strack, "wore a yellow taffeta gown made with a bertha collar and a full skirt. She carried lavender carnations." Yes, pretty fancy for a bunch of South Omaha meatpackers.

The newlyweds were feted by friends and family in the church hall, drove to the Rocky Mountains for a honeymoon, then returned to Omaha and got busy building a family. In July 1950, a month before the birth of their first child, Eddie Jr., the couple borrowed $2,500 from Uncle Frank (Darby) Krajicek to buy a building lot at 3901 Polk Street in South Omaha. They paid to have a cinder-block basement built there and lived below-ground as their first three children, Eddie, Colleen, and Ricky, arrived exactly 12 months apart in August 1950, 1951, and 1952. Construction of the above-ground portion of the three-bedroom house began during Helen's pregnancy with me, in 1955. They filled it quickly. Sisters Carol arrived in 1957 and Julie in '60.

The year of my birth brought the first in a series of untimely deaths to the Krajiceks. Uncle Darby, who struggled with alcohol addiction, died in 1955, at age 49. Anna Kopecky Krajicek, our original immigrant ancestor, died five years later after a life that spanned 82 years, 5,000 miles, and an ocean. Eddie was very close to both of them, having spent his formative years in the same household.

The next great tragedy in Eddie's life was a heart-stopper—almost unthinkable, even all these years later. Helen, suffering from severe but undiagnosed anemia, died while giving birth to their seventh and eighth children, twin daughters named Helen and Marie in her honor. She was just 34 years old when she died, on September 25, 1962.

Earlier that summer, Eddie, the pregnant Helen, and their six children took a weekend car trip. In retrospect, the journey seems to have been a form of foreboding. First, we drove 90 miles northwest from Omaha through the Iowa countryside to tiny Vail, where we visited Daisy, her daughter Jean, and sundry relatives from the Chandler family. We then drove on, traveling another 100 miles north to West Bend, Iowa, a small town near the Minnesota border. There we spent a couple of hours touring the Grotto of the Redemption, an expansive, European-style Catholic shrine pieced together in the early 1900s from gleaming semiprecious stones — azurite, agates, quartz, topaz, and others — collected by a German immigrant priest, Paul Matthias Dobberstein. The grotto had become a destination for devout Catholic tourists, but I can't really explain why we went. Yes, we attended Catholic school, went to Mass, and recited prayers of thanks before meals. But our parents did not seem the sort of Catholics who would have embarked on a pilgrimage — especially with six unruly kids in tow.

I suspect it was Helen's idea. In about 1957, she and Eddie purchased a high-quality film camera and used it to shoot hundreds of feet of footage of their children. A number of those soundless films survived for decades, thanks to sturdy canisters. Most contain standard home-movie fare — the kids posing in pajamas, opening Christmas gifts, frolicking in the yard. But one canister contained footage, shot by Helen, of our visit to the grotto. It is a precious time capsule, needless to say. Our father shows up in the frame, looking awkward beside one of the grotto chapels. The older kids appear restrained — or bored. The lack of sound gives the moving images an eeriness, like a horror film just before something awful happens. And so it was.

Remarkably, I also now have photographic evidence of our visit to the Chandlers in Vail, the first stop of that trip. I was just 6 years old at the time but have vivid memories of the excursion. I wasn't certain on the details of where and when, but I knew we had visited a relative's farm in Iowa, people named Dicey and Jean. I mentioned this while speaking with Janean Haukap, Daisy's granddaughter. I hadn't made the connection, but it turned out she was the daughter of that very couple—Lawrence (Dicey) Nelson and his wife Jean, Daisy's younger daughter. Janean had been there during our visit, as a teenager. She still lives not far from Vail, and our conversation jogged her memory. She rummaged through boxes in her attic, and a week later a collection of photos from the Krajicek visit in 1962 arrived in the mail. They had been stored for six decades by the Chandlers. The photos helped me date the trip—and piece together its connection to the grotto visit. The film and photographs might have been the last images taken of our mother. She looked exhausted, frankly.

All of this prompted me to go back and take another look at the history of the Grotto of the Redemption. Old Father Dobberstein left no real explanation of what motivated him to build his Iowa colossus. The shrine's materials say that he "was confident that the finished project would speak for itself." But the priest did say that he was moved by a particular entry in the Bible's Book of Psalms. It says, in essence, *Lord, I will be satisfied when I awake and see your face.* I am not a person of faith; when I lost my mother, I also lost any inclination to believe that we are part of a just, moral, and orderly theology. But my mother apparently did believe that, so I hope the psalm was her destiny. She gave her life to procreation. She deserved an afterlife.

Somehow, our remarkable father held the family together. The twins spent their first year under the care of nuns at a Catholic orphanage in Omaha. Their father visited them several times a week,

The Krajicek Family and Julie and Colleen Krajicek, Vail, Iowa, 1962

and we siblings were packed into the station wagon for trips to see the twins on many Sunday afternoons. They came home to us 12 months later. Helen's mother, Eileen, tended to the twins (and the rest of us) during those first years, with help from her sisters, Dorothy and Eileen, and several of Helen's girlfriends.

Just as life was on Polk Street was beginning to stabilize in the mid-1960s, Eddie lost his job as the packinghouses began pulling out of South Omaha in a union-busting tactic to move to rural locations where they could hire cheaper labor and increase profits. He transitioned to another form of family business and opened the Lodge Bar & Café, in a small town south of Omaha near a cluster of residential lakes along the Platte River. It grew into a successful enterprise—due entirely to our father's tireless work and winning way with customers. The Lodge was our family's homeport for 50 years.

The letters to Hazel ceased after Eddie's Navy stretch, as he was consumed by these more urgent matters. He did speak with her by phone occasionally, and Hazel visited Omaha a few times. She made one of those trips to attend the funeral of her second son. Connie Krajicek, after marrying and fathering three children, lost himself to alcohol in the late 1960s. He died of liver disease in November 1970.

A year before his brother died, our father was fortunate enough to find a new love—a women open to the frightening possibility of inheriting eight children. He married Beverly Broome on June 14, 1969, and they would add a son, Bill, to the family three years later. By then, Hazel had finally settled into her own lasting relationship. She split with "Big" Bob Beron after about five years and took up with a divorced Detroit autoworker named Frederic Fisch. The son of Polish immigrant parents, Fred had grown up on a farm in north-central Michigan. Like many thousands of others, he gravitated as a young man to Detroit, 175 miles away, and the Motor City's plentiful, well-paying assembly line jobs.

Hazel and Fred hooked up in Detroit, drawn together at least in part by their mutual lust for whiskey. I would bet that they met in a saloon. Hazel, a robustly built woman, must have had a thing for big men. Ed Krajicek was tall and strapping, and Beron's "big" nickname suggests he was the same. Photos of Hazel with Fisch show him as a large, sturdy fellow, as well.

They were married on June 6, 1947, in Harrison, Michigan. He was 41, two years older than Hazel, and each been to the altar (or the court clerk) before. Fred had two young sons, Robert, 12, and

Fred and Hazel Fisch, Vail, Iowa, 1956

Ronald, 9, born during an eight-year marriage to a local Michigan woman, Lenora Wylie, that had ended in divorce in 1943. Relatives told me that Fred and Hazel split time between an apartment in Detroit and a country farmhouse on McCulloch Road, a mile from the small town of Gladwin, Michigan. Fred continued to work at a Chrysler factory in the city, so they would commute together by bus, spending weekdays in Detroit and weekends in Gladwin, where Fred raised cattle as a side job. Hazel did not work. Compared to the family bedlam in South Omaha, they seemed to have lived a relatively sedate life—no family homicides, no moonshining, no runaway spouses.

But Hazel's lifelong problems with alcohol burst into full bloom in Gladwin, where she became a notorious town drunk. I had a frank and honest conversation about her life in Michigan with Jane Fisch Bulmer, a retired nurse and niece of Fred Fisch. I asked for her impressions of Hazel.

"She was quite a lady," Jane told me, with a little laugh. "I'm sure you know that she was an alcoholic, and I think that played a large role in her life. My family would stop by their farmhouse after church on Sunday to visit, but we never stayed too long—an hour at the most. There would be empty whiskey bottles everywhere, on every shelf, in every nook. Kessler was her brand. She always carried a pint in her apron pocket or her coat, so it was always right at hand. She could be very entertaining and was fun until she got mean, so my folks made sure we left before it got to that point. But I can tell you that she was kicked out of every bar in town, to give you an idea of what she was like when she drank. The story goes that she liked to throw things."

That jibes with the Krajicek family lore that Hazel left Ed Krajicek with permanent hearing loss when she conked him on the head with a table lamp. Fred and Hazel's relationship lasted three decades. I asked Jane why Fred would have endured her.

"Well, Uncle Fred liked his whiskey, too," she said, "although I think the drinking had more of a negative effect on her. He had the Chrysler job plus his cattle, so he had to be responsible. But they were a funny pair. They would fight like cats and dogs, and then they would turn around an hour later, and Hazel would be sitting right up next to him in the car, like they were teenagers."

The Fisch family has a collection of stories about Hazel's antics—including the time she passed out drunk on a bus ride home from Detroit and ended up stranded 150 miles north of Gladwin, in Mackinaw City. But Jane said she wanted to emphasize that Hazel could be a kind and fierce ally, like the time she stormed into the local high school in protest in the early '70s after Jane's sister, Carol, was suspended for attending school braless. "Our mother died when we were young, and Hazel was always very good to Carol and me," Jane said. "She really took Carol under her wing, especially."

* * *

After her marriage to Fred, Hazel continued to make occasional trips back to Iowa and Kansas City to see her sisters, to whom she remained close—though not close enough, apparently. *"Say, why don't you write?"* Leafy groused in a letter in May 1946, four months after their mother died of gas poisoning. Daisy and Leafy must have coordinated an assault on Hazel. That same month, Daisy wrote, *"Why don't you write? I know you have time. Or even call. I've tried twice to call you. Call and charge it here, will you? Are you coming to visit soon? Try and come."*

Photographic proof shows that Fred and Hazel did finally make it back to see her sisters, in July of 1956. Janean Haukap told me that she recalls several of Hazel's visits to see Daisy, known to her family as "Ma," in Iowa in the 1950s and '60s. She left an indelible image. "Oh, I remember your grandma," Janean said. "She would come to

Fred and Hazel Fisch with Daisy, Vail, Iowa, 1956

Vail and visit Daisy. Both ladies were a piece of work! Ma, oh my God, she had a mouth on her. I can still hear her saying goddamn-sonofabitch, like it was one word."

Daisy and Hazel always had one priority during those visits, Janean told me.

"As kids we didn't spend a lot of time around Hazel when she was here because they believed children were to be seen (for 5 minutes) and not heard," she said. "Unfortunately, I only remember how much she and Ma drank. They spent most of their time together in a bar. They both liked their alcohol. She and Ma were both lovely ladies; they just liked to drink. Never ever did I see them mean or verbally abusive. They just enjoyed their whiskey."

As Michigan's Jane Bulmer testified, Hazel apparently soured with age. She and Fred spent 30 years together, from their first meeting in 1946 until his sudden death from a heart attack in 1976. Hazel struggled financially with Fred gone, and her dutiful surviving son stepped in to help, of course. The final letters in Hazel's little suitcase were written in the year following Fred's death. They were brief and businesslike—yet showed touches of Eddie's abiding kindness.

March 14, 1977

Dear Mom:

Sending check and some pictures. I have your checks. When you need anything write me or call.

It is 70 degrees today and sunny. We have had two inches of rain lately and things are turning green. Hope to take Billy fishing next week. Everyone is fine and sends you their love. I called Daisy last week—also Jessie Kirk [a Chandler cousin]. *They will write or call you.*

Colleen is going to have her baby any day now. This will be my third grandchild. Carol will have one later this year, too.

Love, Ed

May 10, 1977

Dear Ma:

Now that you are a member of the jet set I hope California isn't too tame for you. [She had flown to California to live with her stepson, Ronald Fisch, and his wife, Joyce.]

I am pleased you are so busy. It's the best thing for you. Sure hope you can get Supplemental Social Security. Have Joyce try there. Yes, Ma, you should pay board and room. I have sent Ron a check already.

I'll call Daisy and let her know. She will probably call. All is fine here. I hope you like your new doctor and your health is fine.

Ma, I hope you really like California and being with Ron and Joyce. They are two very nice people. Sounds as if all the kids love Grandma, too.

Haven't had a chance to fish yet, but hope to go to Canada June 24. We send our love and will call in a couple of weeks. Do what the doctor tells you.

Love, Ed

November 9, 1977

Dear Ma:

Here is your mail. I have more checks when you need them.

Has Grace got you lined up for SSI as yet?

It is snowing and blowing like hell here for the last 16 hours. The wind never stops it seems. Everyone is fine. Bev stays busy teaching piano at the Southroads Mall, and business is good, so I have more to do than I want to.

Sorry I don't write more often but I never did. Time to get things going for dinner time. Bye for now.

Love, Ed

'Paid in Full'

RONALD AND JOYCE FISCH'S GRACIOUS ATTEMPT to help care for Hazel at their California home did not work. She was back in Michigan after just a few months. She had been diagnosed with breast cancer sometime after Fred died and was undergoing treatment. Perhaps she felt more comfortable in her adopted state. She must have felt isolated, living in the California suburbs. And from her stepson's perspective, the chronically boozy Hazel would have been a lot to handle.

By the spring of 1980, the cancer had spread to her liver, and her life was nearing its end. Hazel's final address was as humble as those of her childhood in Wichita and South Omaha. She was living at 225 Cedar Avenue, the busy main drag of Gladwin, Michigan, in a tiny apartment above a commercial storefront. As her cancer advanced, she was removed to a hospital in Midland, Michigan, a small city 35 miles south of Gladwin. When she checked in, she gave her son Eddie as her emergency contact.

He received the phone call announcing his mother's death on May 20, 1981. Liver failure was the immediate cause, as a consequence of the metastasized cancer, according to the attending physician, Dr. William Cline. Hazel was the first of the sisters to go, but the others soon followed—Leafy, in December 1982 at age 78, Daisy in March 1985 at 82.

The end of his own sad drinking life had come early for their brother, John. He had returned to Omaha in the late 1940s, after more than a decade in Detroit. He reconnected with his wife and fathered a fourth child, Marygrace, born in 1949. In September 1950, Chandler landed the family name back in the news when he was accused in the beating death amid a "wine-caused fog" of a fellow drunk, Joe Plavan Jr., whose body was found in a weedy ballfield at the South 30th Street projects. Stories in the *World-Herald* said Chandler woke up beside the battered body of Plavan but could not remember anything due to chronic blackouts from drinking and the head injury from his teenage car wreck. For several days, authorities weighed bringing homicide charges against John. In the weeks or months before Plavan's death, Chandler had had another psychiatric episode that landed him in the state mental hospital. According to the Omaha police, he had been released just days before going on the bender that culminated in his zonked-out proximity to the battered body of his drinking buddy. It would have been a difficult prosecution, so the district attorney took the shrewd route and simply returned Chandler to psychiatric care, in lieu of criminal charges. I don't know how long he was locked up, but when released John left his Omaha family yet again and returned to Detroit. Back in his old haunts, he once again plodded along in the same alcoholic rut. By the late 1950s, he was living in a homeless shelter as his health failed. He was hospitalized in Detroit in the summer of 1959 and died there on August 30. Doctors cited pulmonary edema—fluid on the lungs—as the cause of death, but that condition typically is related to other problems such as pneumonia, heart, liver, or kidney disease—or brain trauma. As a 10-year-old child, Marygrace also answered a phone call from Michigan announcing a parent's death. John Chandler was 52 years old when he died. "I barely knew him," Marygrace told me, "so I can't really tell you what kind of person he was. But to the day she died, despite everything he did to us by running off, my mother defended John as a good man who lived with difficult circumstances." In a note to me a few days later, Marygrace added, "I don't know if my father was stable enough to provide for the family. I believe he had very good intentions but just could not carry them out. It really is something, though, that he came back 17 years later and my mom and dad got back together. It was loving."

His body was returned to South Omaha for a funeral and burial at St. Mary's Cemetery at 36th and Q Streets. Among those who signed the guest register were Eddie and Helen Krajicek. An exclamation point to John Chandler's tragic life came about a week later. His eldest daughter, Rita, her husband, Frank Mickells, and their young son, Michael, were driving home to California after the funeral when their Mercury automobile was involved in horrendous crash in Gallup, New Mexico. All three perished.

* * *

My father and his wife, Beverly, flew to Michigan for Hazel's funeral, held in Gladwin three days after her death. She was buried in a rural cemetery not far from where she and Fred had lived. Eddie paid for his mother's sendoff, a total of $2,372.20 to the Hall Funeral Home in Gladwin. Years later, Beverly found the receipt, inscribed "Paid in Full" by proprietor Thomas Hall, in a small collection of documents that included Hazel's death certificate. It delineated the expenses: $1,750 for "casket and services," $345 for a burial vault, $125 for cemetery fees, $62.40 for flowers, $48.80 in state sales taxes, $25 to the clergyman, $16 for three certified copies of the death certificate.

Grace Chandler and children John and Hazel, South Omaha, 1941

Dad loved paying bills — or rather, he loved eliminating debts. He was obsessive about it, so I suspect he was quietly satisfied as he flew home from Gladwin, gripping the little suitcase of letters and a funeral receipt. He had taken care of his mother by wiping clean her financial slate as she departed this life.

Somehow during his alienated childhood and tragic adulthood, Hazel's eldest son was imbued with character and conscience. He showed his mother to the very end that there was literally nothing she could do to turn him away from her. During reflective moments, he would sometimes speak about Hazel with Beverly, who told me that his message was clear but kindhearted: *I don't respect her, but she is my mother, and therefore I love her.*

I subscribe to the idea that love, like respect, ought to be earned, not given. But my unselfish father clearly did not see it that way. For him, the love of Hazel was his duty — like paying bills. About six weeks before he died in 1992, my father and Beverly drove out to visit me at the weekend home I had purchased in the Catskill Mountains, a few hours from New York City. On the way east, they took a seven-hour, 450-mile detour off Interstate 90 to visit Hazel's grave. I asked Beverly not long ago what the cemetery visit had meant to him. "He just wanted to see it, to be there with her," she said. "He stood quietly for a few minutes, and we were back on our way. When I think about it now, it seems like he was a completing a circle of some sort — a circle of his life. Of course, I didn't foresee that he would leave us just a month or two later. But it's almost as though he knew. And he wanted to stand there at the end with the person who was with him at the beginning."

I had a conversation recently with Sandy Krajicek Lim, dad's cousin whose birth was announced in an early letter to Hazel. She knew Eddie and Connie as well anyone, having grown up next door. She made a point about something that I had been mulling over since I began reading their childhood letters.

"I remember once that I was in a car with Connie and Delores, his wife," Sandy told me. "She had just had a miscarriage, and I can't tell you how sweet and sympathetic Connie was toward that poor woman. It was so touching, and I remember it so well to this day. See, Connie was just like your dad, very warm. Whatever faults they may or may not have had, they were both sweet boys who grew up into sweet, sympathetic men. It's amazing they turned out the way they did, with all that they went through as children. I mean, how did that happen?"

* * *

It's true. Eddie was sweet and sympathetic. He was also sentimental. He cried easily, especially over kindnesses paid to him. He could laugh so hard that his shoulders would shake. He snored like a bear. He was a gentleman. He was clever and smart, and he could be delightfully goofy. On his treasured trout-fishing trips with his buddies, they would sit around a campfire on the banks of the Green River in Utah, pass around a gallon jug of cheap wine, and sing "Jesus Loves Me"—because it was the only song lyrics they knew. I'm sorry that Hazel missed out on seeing those sides of her son. He was a wonderful man. And I'm sorry that he was unable to share his warm and loving self with her.

In the hospital in 1992, just before his heart gave out, my father was lying in his bed and giving me detailed directions on paying a bill that had been weighing on his mind. I told him I would take care it—and that he should stop fretting.

"Dad, you worry too much," I told him.

He said, "I probably do, but I've always had a lot to worry about."

"Please just stop it for now," I said.

He was not the sort of man to indulge himself with self-analysis, but he said something that surprised me.

"Fear of failure is probably why I worry," he said.

Eddie Krajicek didn't want to let down the people who loved him — almost certainly psychological baggage from Hazel's abandonment. And he surely did not. He was determined to succeed, even when faced with life crises that would have prompted most of us to buckle at the knees. He didn't complain, didn't waste time wringing his hands. But he also didn't forget where he came from. Beverly says that he would occasionally drive down South 23rd Street and point out the little house where he took his first steps, where he welcomed home his baby brother, where his family was intact for a few precious years, and where — through some miracle — he came to understand that a commitment meant forever to him, even if it didn't for his mother. It's interesting that he did not encourage a relationship between his mother and his children. I think he was protecting us from her.

At the end of my snooping, I haven't uncovered a revelatory rationale for why Hazel's life unraveled. But I do understand that her personal story was more complicated than the one-dimensional "she's-a-drunk" trope. Yes, booze framed her life. But she was also a troubled and exasperating woman who came from a challenging genetic, economic, and moral background. To me, her people were wanderers in so many ways, and she carried on that tradition.

One of the many striking lines in the Krajicek boys' letters was my father's reply in 1947 when Hazel wrote to him in Pearl Harbor to reveal that she had just remarried, to Fred Fisch. Eddie wrote, "You deserve all of the happiness in the world, mom." Seven decades after that exchange, I wanted to find out whether Hazel was content in Michigan — more so than she might have been had she stayed in Nebraska with her first husband and two boys. I asked Jane Bulmer, Fred Fisch's niece, whether Hazel had found the happiness that her son said she deserved. She paused for several moments before she answered.

"Honestly, I have to say no," Jane said, speaking softly. "I don't think she was truly happy, and I can tell you why I say that. When she drank, she would cry—and I mean really sob. She would get so sad. I remember that so well . . . I do think her alcoholism got to her in the end. But I also think that as she got older, she felt more and more regret. She would talk about Eddie quite a lot, and I think she regretted what she had done, leaving her sons. I think her sadness came from that deep, deep regret."

I asked my stepmother, Beverly, for her thoughts on Hazel. She was better acquainted with her than my siblings and I, having met her several times, including when Hazel stayed at her home while in Omaha to attend Connie's funeral. She also listened to my father talk about his mother—something he rarely did with me. "It still boggles my mind to think about what Hazel did," Beverly told me. "My goodness, imagine the heartache she caused to her sons and the rest of her family by that decision. I just think that she could not be a responsible human being to her own sons. For whatever reasons that we'll never really know, she just wasn't capable of giving love and commitment like a normal mother would."

That seems to be an indisputable endquote to Hazel's story. She was anything but normal. I'm sorry that Hazel didn't get the help she needed; alcoholism is a disease, not a character flaw, and it consumed her. Today, she might have been tracked toward treatment—which may or may not have worked, of course. But she came of age in a much different era. I think that my grandmother understood her flaws and decided, consciously or not, that while she needed Eddie and Connie in her life, she determined sometime in 1936 that they were better off without her around. Sadly, for all concerned, she was probably right.

Acknowledgements

I PESTERED MANY RELATIVES in researching this book, including Beverly Krajicek, Sandra Krajicek Lim, and Robert and Janean Haukap. Each was patient and honest in sharing their recollections. Special thanks to Bob Haukap, who has assembled a great deal of information on the Chandlers—and invited the enmity of his in-laws for his dogged snooping. I admire him for that. He would have made a good reporter. Early in my research, Bob told me, "You better have a sense of humor if you're trying to make sense of the Chandler family." I had no idea how true that would be.

Likewise, many thanks to Marygrace Chandler Hansen, the last surviving child of the colorful Chandler siblings. Her father, John Chandler, was a stranger to her, and she has made a valiant, loving attempt to collect the pieces of his broken life. I was moved by her tenacity and resolve.

And this story would have been incomplete had I not gotten lucky enough to speak with Jane Fisch Bulmer, who shared her honest, warts-and-all memories of my grandmother's life in Michigan.

On the production side, a note of thanks for the design of this book by Terry Bradshaw, my talented friend and fellow author. And thanks, as well, to my neighbor Karen Gutliph Graves, a remarkable artist who contributed original illustrations.

Lastly, a second thank you to my stepmother, Beverly, for bringing emotional solace, abiding love, and deep joy to my father, who richly deserved all of that.

About the Author

DAVID J. KRAJICEK HAS BEEN TELLING STORIES for more than 40 years, as an author and newspaperman. A native of South Omaha, Nebraska, he comes from a long line of meatpackers and saloon-keepers—men and women who have told a few stories of their own. Krajicek is among America's most prominent criminal justice journalists, having written a true crime column for the *New York Daily News* for 20 years. He spent a decade as a Columbia

The author and his father, New York City, 1990

University journalism professor and has published widely in leading newspapers and magazines, including *The New York Times* and the *Guardian*. His books include *Mass Killers: Inside the Minds of Men Who Murder*, and *Charles Manson: The Man Who Murdered the Sixties*, both published in 2019 by Arcturus Books of London; the regional best-seller *True Crime: Missouri, The State's Most Notorious Criminal Cases* (Stackpole, 2011), and his acclaimed first book, *Scooped: Media Miss Real Story on Crime While Chasing Sex, Sleaze, and Celebrities* (Columbia University Press, 1998).

Made in the USA
Monee, IL
01 April 2021

63275389R00073